Little Yellow House

Little  Yellow House
Finding Community in a Changing Neighbourhood

CARISSA HALTON

Gutteridge
BOOKS

An Imprint of The University of Alberta Press

Published by

The University of Alberta Press
Ring House 2
Edmonton, Alberta, Canada T6G 2E1
www.uap.ualberta.ca

Copyright © 2018 Carissa Halton.

LIBRARY AND ARCHIVES CANADA
CATALOGUING IN PUBLICATION

Halton, Carissa, 1979-, author
    Little yellow house : finding community in
a changing neighbourhood / Carissa Halton.

Issued in print and electronic formats.
ISBN 978-1-77212-375-3 (softcover). —
ISBN 978-1-77212-427-9 (EPUB). —
ISBN 978-1-77212-428-6 (Kindle). —
ISBN 978-1-77212-429-3 (PDF).

    1. Halton, Carissa, 1979- . 2. Alberta
Avenue (Edmonton, Alta.). 3. Neighborhoods—
Alberta—Edmonton. 4. Community life—
Alberta—Edmonton. 5. Edmonton (Alta.) —
Social conditions. 6. Edmonton (Alta.) —
Economic conditions. I. Title.

FC3696.52.H35 2018   307.76097123'34
C2018-902392-9
C2018-902393-7

First edition, second printing, 2018.
First printed and bound in Canada by Houghton
Boston Printers, Saskatoon, Saskatchewan.
Copyediting and proofreading by
Maya Fowler-Sutherland.

The University of Alberta Press is committed to
protecting our natural environment. As part of
our efforts, this book is printed on Enviro Paper:
it contains 100% post-consumer recycled fibres
and is acid- and chlorine-free.

The University of Alberta Press gratefully
acknowledges the support received for its
publishing program from the Government of
Canada, the Canada Council for the Arts, and
the Government of Alberta through the Alberta
Media Fund.

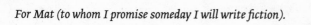

For Mat (to whom I promise someday I will write fiction).

||||||

It is to our great cities' peril that we ignore the lessons contained in the cracked sidewalks, weedy yards, and dejected strip malls of our oldest neighbourhoods.

Contents

Preface

MY HUSBAND, MAT, AND I wanted to live closer to our work in the inner city—he spent his days in three junior high schools supporting kids in government care and I managed programs at a soup kitchen. We wanted to better understand the neighbourhoods where so many of the people we served lived. Plus, we had very little money so we bought a house in Alberta Avenue, which one wealthy art dealer had described to me as "the shitty part of town." It was the part of town where sixty years ago my grandmother had lived with her British mother in a well-run rooming house overlooking the community hall rink where players' skates sliced after pucks. It was the part of town where my grandfather grew up, hanging out in his father's appliance shop after school waiting to be handed an errand. When they heard we'd bought a house in their old neighbourhood they said simply, "You paid how much?"

We were told, "You'll move when you have kids." After Madi, Lily, and then Alistair were born we were told, "You'll move when the kids go to school." About the time our oldest went to the community school, people stopped telling us when we would move from the century-old house that every year required another renovation. We had a bakery and a volunteer-run arts café down the block, and within walking distance there were playgrounds, a library, school and bus stops to downtown. And while we wished there were fewer empty storefronts along the main avenue and fewer johns trolling to buy sex, the elm trees on the boulevard shaded the streets that led to the homes of many of our extended family: close enough that if, say, I went into sudden labour in the middle of the night a relative could literally run over. In short, we discovered shitty is how you see it.

1

Avoid This Place
at Night

A FEW YEARS AFTER WE MOVED TO the neighbourhood I typed "where to eat on 118 Ave" into my search engine and this review popped up:

> 118th Avenue in Edmonton stretches on for quite a long way, but the most dangerous part is from approximately 97th Street to 30th Street. [It's the stretch between 101st Street and 82nd Street that is known as Alberta Avenue.] A lot of the neighbourhoods that fall along the avenue are low income and very run down. There are prostitutes all over the place, with their pimps not far off I'm sure. There are lots of drug dealers/gangsters, and their preferred mode of transportation is stolen bicycles. If you ever see a grown man on a bike that is way too small for him in this area, that is probably why. There are lots of pawn shops and seedy bars along this avenue as well.
>
> I don't want to make it sound too too bad, because there are a few good restaurants and bakeries along here, but it's a place you should definitely avoid at night."
>
> —"118th Avenue-Hookers-Drugs and Thugs" by Karlie85

We've had our garage broken into a couple times over a decade and the first time, thieves with a massive truck broke the flimsy latch and stole an air compressor, leaving clear dually tire prints in the snow on the back cement pad. The second time our garage was hit by thieves they stole an air compressor, again.

"Are air compressors used in some kind of drug operation?" I asked Mat.

"It's just a tool that gets good return when pawned," Mat said as he walked a couple of blocks to the closest pawn shop and bought a different one back. It was a heavy mother of a compressor. However, just to be safe, Mat bought a long length of chain and secured it to the garage wall. Whoever wanted this tool would need to have bolt cutters *and* a truck.

When we moved into the community, people always talked about the crime. Friends told me their realtors recommended they not look at homes in the area and, if one is a tourist, many website reviewers helpfully direct you to other parts of the city.

I don't walk very comfortably at night on 118th Avenue, but I haven't felt comfortable walking at night in any of the neighbourhoods in which I've lived. Even in the rural Rocky Mountain town where we grew up, Mat and I would walk along the dark gravel roads winding into the backcountry and I never completely relaxed. There were always bears, and unknown stalkers in the occasional passing car. In the city, the threat is serial rapists or sadists and like bears, they can walk kilometres in a day and where they were last sighted is not always helpful because the next day they would be somewhere else.

2

Better to Call 311

IT WAS THAT SEASON AGAIN when the dark creeps into our evenings and steals the green from the trees. Mat folded laundry downstairs, the girls ran around our house naked, and I was washing the dinner dishes when I heard breaking glass from the alley. The sound came again through the open patio door. Into the near-dark backyard I moved as fast as my pregnant body would allow towards the alley and saw a white, older-model Caravan idling behind my neighbour's lot. Stepping out further, I spotted the source of the sound.

A short man with the belly of Santa Claus was dumping twenty-litre pails of what sounded like glass onto the back lot of a newly built house. It had replaced a single-storey cottage that we had watched being dismantled first by its joists, then walls, then brick foundation. Most clearly I remember a gold-coloured refrigerator slumped in the front loader's bucket, its cord so recently torn from a socket that it swung like a ticking pendulum.

When the demolition trucks left, only a low brick wall remained at the front, its wrought iron gate swung open over a cracking sidewalk that led to a hole strewn with insulation and migrating shreds of tar paper. Eventually a crew arrived with a truck whose highest point stretched taller than the elm trees on the boulevard. It emptied a steady stream of cement into the basement.

A new house rose along with a corresponding mound of garbage at the alley. There were blocks of rough concrete, broken glass and drywall mud buckets. Eventually someone added a microwave to the top of the pile. Its door opened with the wind to leer at traffic bumping slowly over alley potholes.

Anywhere in my city one can call 311 if such a garbage pile persists and, if I ever see a short, pot-bellied man with an unbuttoned Hawaiian shirt and crucifix on a gold chain emptying twenty-litre buckets of glass in the back alley again, I will call 311. However, when I saw the man in the shadows dumping his garbage in my alley, I was pregnant and incapable of considering non-confrontational options like phone calls to friendly city bylaw officers.

"Excuse me?" I raised my voice. It had the inflection of a demand, not a request. He turned towards the truck, and grabbed another pail. Did he really just have the nerve to ignore me?

"Excuse me, sir!" I was yelling now. Moving, not yet charging, towards him so he could better hear me. "Sir, what are you doing?"

He finally turned and shrugged a non-verbal, *What? This?*

Out loud, he said, "Sorry," and, "were you talking to me?"

"Yes, why are you dumping glass in my back alley?"

"Oh, no, it's not glass. This is tile. See?" He gestured for me to move closer to inspect the pile. His confidence that this mattered made my reaction so much worse: "Tile? How exactly is tile any different than glass? Can I tell you about the kids that ride their bikes back here? About the fact that my kids live twenty feet from a very attractive, climbable pile of *garbage* that now has not just glass, not just a microwave, not just huge bits of broken cement and rebar and who knows what else."

I pointed to my home. "Kids live here."

I pointed to my neighbours' home, where the kids play video games inside fourteen hours a day. "And there."

I pointed to the home where five kids live with their grandma and somehow all fit in the cab of her rusted red truck. "And there are five more here."

I pointed finally to a home where the Greek man died and which had been vacant for months: "And there. Kids live everywhere along this back alley and you want to come and bring your shit tiles and just add them the rest of this shit pile?"

His hands were raised in surrender, but I had no flashlight. I had no police back up. All I had was a raging righteousness partly inspired by the incredible estrogen and extra blood teeming through my veins. It felt so good that I kept going, and moving forward I ventured into sarcasm. "Sir, shall I draw you a map? Don't you know where the landfill is? Because it's actually outside of the city. This is the middle of the city. This is the middle of my bloody neighbourhood and I'm not going to let more of your not-glass-tiles get dumped on that pile where they become a 911 waiting to happen. Is that what you need, a map?"

"This is my boss's house. He told me to just bring my tiles here. I'm working on one of his houses down on the east end."

"Oh, your boss owns this house that is taking forever to finish? Well I'd like to talk to him because he is building this pile *way* faster than the house."

It was about this time that my husband, Mat, heard the shrill sounds of a lady in what he thought was a drunken dispute. He paused to make sure no one was getting hurt, then he paused again to make sure he'd heard what he thought he'd heard. That lady was in fact his pregnant wife using a voice reserved only for the animals after they had tracked garden mud onto her new white chairs. He grabbed his flashlight and, followed by his daughters, marched out the patio doors, down the deck stairs, past the garage and out the back gate.

Tile Man suddenly found himself surrounded. Two blond, naked little girls in bare feet stared at him disapprovingly. Mat aimed a flashlight squarely at his license plate. Our neighbour and his dog were finishing their walk and came at him from behind. Then there was me still raving. It was at this time that his *What, this?* posture melted.

He offered to never do it again. He offered to detour to the dump himself. He offered to talk to his boss—no, he could not give me the boss's number but he would certainly talk to his boss for me. He said he would be going now and as he shut his door and drove away the kids pulled at our legs. "Why were you yelling at him?"

I sighed and hedged, "It's a long story, girls."

Mat suggested I explain that long story to them as they went to bed. It did not take me long to feel embarrassed at how loudly I swore and how confrontational I had been in public. However they did not accept my contrition. They took on my righteous anger and asked, "Mommy, can you believe he was making our neighbourhood ugly? Someone should talk to the police."

As their questions and blinks slowed, a knock sounded on the front door and Mat left his post putting the dishes away to find Tile Man standing nervously on our deck. His Portuguese accent drifted through the heat registers to the bedroom and the conversation's tone was low, civil, level; occasionally, there was pleading. When Tile Man left, I rolled with zero decorum out of the narrow single bed where one kid was already asleep. On finding Mat I saw him roll his eyes before he recounted the conversation that started and ended with, "Please, please don't call the government."

The tiles remained on the pile that grew for another few months until finally a dump truck arrived, closely followed by a moving truck that emptied the belongings of a very quiet family into the brand-new, bland box of a house.

3

Drug Houses
Make Bad Neighbours

MY MOM AND DAD moved into Alberta Avenue a few years after we had my second daughter, Lily, and they settled six blocks north of us in a 1950s bungalow. As they readied to make the move from their small town to our big city, Mom asked me and Mat, "Now that we'll be so close, would you mind terribly if we had the kids for a sleepover one night a week?"

Mat and I paused and pretended to think about it until we noticed that she looked worried, so we tripped over each other to say emphatically, "No, we wouldn't mind at all."

Their neighbourhood was developed a half century later than ours and the lots are often wide with room for more duplexes and bungalows, and there is the occasional front driveway that emerges from a 1990s garage. Some of the houses look tired and depressed by their middle age, but many have been maintained with regular paint and elaborate gardens. The north-south streets end in cul de sacs where a ten-foot cement block fence muffles the engine and brake noise of the Yellowhead highway that can take you to Jasper's Rockies or the Canadian Shield.

It's a community with a safe feel. One week in the middle of summer, however, Dad answered a knock at the door and faced the business card of a police officer in jeans, a T-shirt and leather loafers who strolled through the living room, dining room, then to the back window above the kitchen sink.

"We're just keeping an eye on the house across the alley, there." He pointed at the garage where the two guys who lived there "fixed cars" that never seemed to get fixed. The detective said nothing more as he left. A few weeks later, I would pick the kids up from their sleepover and be rerouted when I turned down the neighbouring street and cop cars were everywhere along with a SWAT team van. They had busted the house and my parents did not seem any the wiser.

IIIII

Drug houses are not always as subtle as this one. When we first moved in, they were a source of great concern and frequent conversation in the stores, the parks, and neighbourly back alley chats. In the mail we got brochures on how to spot a drug house, though most neighbours did not need any help; the obvious ones seemed ringed with an invisible force field that inspired you to cross the street, or look to the ground, or walk faster as you pulled out your cell phone for a fake call. On some of my walking routes, the few I gave a wide berth had security cameras at the front door and grass that sprouted seeds it was so long. The folks inside rarely saw how badly the yard needed to be mowed because of the flannel sheet set of the solar system taped to their windows.

For instances like these, there were even more detailed brochures on how to deal with said drug house, as well as magnets with "Report a Drug House" phone numbers. Residents were advised not to engage occupants or visitors to the home, to report all suspicious activity to the police, and record, record, record. For many folks who lived next to such a house and who did not require the convenience of their illicit services, they had the unpleasant task of recording for what felt like a very long time. People like Christy and Darcy Morin who I met in our time as baristas at the volunteer-run arts café on 118th Avenue. They had moved into the neighbourhood in 1994 but then spent the next ten years asking themselves the question, "Should we just go?" Christy's parents advised them to leave and on calling the police after one particularly scary exchange with a neighbour, the officer told Christy, "Ma'am, you sound like a very reasonable person. Can I advise you to just move?"

Their home was otherwise perfect. A sweet, 1950s bungalow with gingerbread siding and coved ceilings, it had a ceramic fireplace that blasted heat adorably but inefficiently. The place had charm and a big backyard for their growing family. It also had a basement suite that, paired with the affordable price they paid for the property, allowed them to pay off their mortgage at a rate they otherwise could not have imagined.

From their perfect little house, however, they watched grown men get drunk on the neighbouring house's peeling roof. They heard the hilarity of the initial high, then felt the anger and despair with which it ended. Knife fights, dog fights, child abuse, drug use. It was an ever-changing crowd of tenants coming in and out but with every renter came the same problems.

The landlord was a man named Sam. They knew his name from the handmade "For Rent" signs that he taped to the front fence every time another tenant skipped town without paying up. They knew his number from the same sign and, after calls to the police began feeling like throwing energy into a black hole, the Morins began to call Sam's cell too.

"Hi, Sam, it's Christy and it's one in the morning. Just letting you know that your tenants are jumping off the roof again."

"Hi Sam, it's Darcy. It's Sunday at six AM and your tenants stole our car and now they've just keyed our rental that replaced the stolen one."

"Hi Sam, it's Christy. It's Tuesday afternoon and your tenant seems to have stabbed his brother on the front steps."

Sometimes when Sam's wife would answer, they would appeal to her for the sake of their two quickly growing children. "Can you imagine your grandchildren living next to such a house?"

Often, Sam would scrawl messages on their shared fence: "Thanks REPORTER Christy." Reporters, like the cops and social workers, are not often trusted in this community, but what else was she to do? "Move," was the advice.

||||

On New Year's Eve, just after midnight, Darcy ran out to the car to get a bag he forgot when he found himself face to face with the most recent neighbour looming above him. "You guys are calling the five-oh, aren't you?" he said. "It *is* you and I know it."

"Hey man, let's talk about this."

"If you call the police again, I swear, I know when your kids are in your yard and when I let my two Dobermans on those kids, you won't recognize them. You hear? You will not recognize them."

"We just want peace," said Darcy.

"Don't give me that shit. You heard me."

Christy watched from the door and was unable to hear. However, she started shaking as the man stalked away. They wept and prayed that night. They called the police and were advised that no charges could be laid because Darcy was not threatened with a visible weapon. When her dad heard the story, he immediately started to look for real estate on the south side near the home she grew up in, in a cement-tracked suburb with wide lots and front curb garbage pick-up. They both agreed it might be best to leave.

||||

Christy told me later that the next evening when the kids were safely in bed, Darcy headed out to buy a roast. On his way to the meat aisle, his phone began flashing with calls but he did not hear it because he had gotten side-tracked listening to sample CDs.

Christy's sister was left with no other choice than to leave voice mails: "Darcy, you need to call Christy. Get home. Something's happening over there. I was on the phone with her and some guys from next door are banging on the doors. She says there are at least five guys. I can hear them yelling."

"Darcy, please call me."

As often as she called Darcy, Christy's sister was trying to get a response from the police. Every time she called they told her that they couldn't help her if the incident wasn't happening to her. "But she's been threatened by these men who told her that if she calls the police again her kids will be hurt," she said.

Sorry. No luck. Christy had to be the rat. Again.

With shaking fingers, Christy found the beat cop's number as unfriendly men gestured from her front lawn. Over the last few years, the beat cops had begun to change the relationship between the community and the police. They rode their bikes and walked the avenues. They were not there to bust anyone, or ticket them. They got to know the kids whose instinct to hide at first sight of their uniforms lessened and they got to know homeowners, tenants, folks with no homes, and addicts. The beat cops, if they gave you their number, could be reached directly.

That night Christy's contact was working and when Darcy turned onto his street with the roast in the passenger seat, his heart stopped. The red and blue lights flashed purple in his brain as he raced to his home where his huge, gang-member neighbours were at differing stages of arrest. There was an ambulance preparing to take one of them to the hospital and it was he who had been the reason for the frantic visit that Christy had misunderstood as threatening. Their earlier threats had spun webs in her ears and when they shouted, "Call the police!" a medical emergency was far from her mind. The same fear she had felt the night before had wrapped her until she was nearly frozen.

||||

At that time the police hadn't just improved their community policing techniques with beat cops; they had also started a Derelict Housing Team that partnered with city bylaw and provincial health authorities who wield powerful health legislation. Instead of shutting the problem properties down for drug violations that required a lot more proof for conviction, they were using other means to force landlords to either sell or manage their properties better. Across the city more and more drug houses were being shut down for uninspiring reasons like rodent infestations and open sewage.

Sometimes landlords like Sam simply did not care who they rented to. They'd bought their properties for so little and paid it off so many times that they didn't have an investment that needed protecting. In fact, problem tenants often meant that landlords saved on expensive upgrades like new flooring in the rotting bathroom or grounded electrical, because they knew no tenant would complain. Sometimes landlords were more sinister. Gangs and other fraudsters saw benefit in colonizing the houses with tenants who bought and sold their dope. As a house became increasingly damaged from parties and fights, blood and bad highs, they flipped the house back and forth between themselves, slapping on cheap siding or patching the visibly shitty shingles. So on top of problems like "Drug House" and "Bad Landlord" one could also apply the term "Mortgage Fraud."

Only a couple of weeks after the incident, the Derelict Housing Team issued so many health violations on Sam's house that he chose to sell instead of fix it.

To Christy and Darcy's surprise, the man who bought the property didn't demolish the tiny, crooked home, but instead jacked it up and poured a foundation. He rewired and dry walled and roofed. They thought he was crazy, until the house sold to a school teacher who brought them cookies and taught their kids to do front rolls.

After the drug house closed Christy and Darcy met other neighbours, many of whom had been too scared to come out. Over time, their gait changed and the customary scurry became more leisurely. They began to make eye contact with one another. They began to wave. Then stop. They breathed deeply as though about to ask a question...then they would ask it like neighbours should feel free to do.

4

Unlikely Space Flight

DANNY HAMER would die by blunt force trauma to the head only ten metres away from one of my favourite places in Alberta Avenue. He died inside an owner-occupied crack house facing south, perpendicular to a ramshackle garage across from the alley. The garage was similar to others in the neighbourhood and sported peeling paint, a cracked driveway and dented door whose mint-coloured paint had faded like lipstick at the end of a long night.

I was four months pregnant with my third child, Alistair, and just as my hips were beginning to slip, I found an incredible massage therapist who worked inside said garage, which belonged to my cousin Gil. Leah lived with Gil in her communal house a few blocks from mine where students, social workers, and contractors lived together in spite of the tiny kitchen. Leah eventually tried to eke out some privacy and converted Gil's sketchy garage into a live-work space. The garage was more of a shed than anything one would trust to house one's car, and I hesitated: *Could I trust my developing baby in it?*

Initial entry provided no more reassurance. Rusted bikes, tools, ski equipment and a dishwasher had all settled in various forms of decomposition and could have been the backdrop of an amateur horror flick. At the back of the garage was a framed room one entered with a small step up through a shortened doorway. Leah slept in the attic loft, invisible from the massage table set in the centre of the ten-by-ten-foot room. Along with an electric heater and a plug-in blanket on the massage table, a dozen tea lights warmed the space. As I lay flat on my belly, surrounded by peeling Dutch scenes of blue children frolicking among windmills to the ennui of David Gray, my body relaxed as Leah teased, cajoled and eased the pressures that left my brain muscle soothed and my tongue loose to blabber about childhood, adulthood, world peace, and inner peace. As I did, my busy life working, parenting, and gestating settled into a context I could handle. As her forearm rolled firmly along my thigh, stress squeezed out like that final millilitre of toothpaste from the tube.

And, *Oh God*! How I needed it as Alistair stretched his body across my insides, shoving my kidneys and bladder out of the way. Children, even before they enter the world, are rude. He just kept growing without regard. Despite his thoughtlessness, Leah thought of him and as he grew she added stiff foam layers to the bed. In each piece she carved out breast inversions and a circle for the babe so that at every stage I could lie comfortably on my front. By eight months I was suspended a foot above the mattress as Leah tucked rolled-up towels under my armpits and around my belly so I was evenly positioned.

Within the comforts of the womb room I was oblivious to the property next door whose occupants had different sleep-wake cycles and certainly a different yard maintenance schedule than I had. The police cars parked outside did not affect the garage-massage magic. This drug house behind Leah's was proving a little trickier to bust because it was owner-occupied, meaning there was no landlord making money off tenants in a rental house with standards bylaw officers could enforce. In this home lived a middle-aged drug user who had inherited the place from his mother and then acquired many *friends*.

Before the murder, I had asked Leah, "Can you lock the garage overhead door?" "Should you attach a dead bolt on the man door?" "What about an intercom to your roomies in the house?" No, no, and no.

"Carissa, I feel perfectly safe," she assured me.

She was, but that was not the case for everyone on the night of October 8, 2011. In the early morning a man with a long list of convictions knocked on the front door across the alley. Daniel Charles Hamer, known as "Nathan" on the street, had stayed in the house on and off that last week and according to police reports, there had been a fight that ended with Hamer dead.

Five metres away from where my massage table was covered in foam shaped like a womb, Hamer's death set a murder record. This was the city's fortieth homicide that year and it made the national news. Yet through the night, Leah slept like a baby.

||||||

The child who would grow up to be Danny Hamer was born Nathan Isbister to a Cree mother and white father in Fort Saskatchewan, Alberta, and was nineteen months old when his mother placed him for adoption. Adopted by the Hamers in 1977, he would be the second oldest of seven siblings and was just three months older than the next closest sister, Dee. The brown-haired child was large for his age, but he did not speak until he was four and so his blond sister interpreted for him. Generally she got it right and the habit would extend far into middle school when she was still answering for him.

As a child of the 1970s and 1980s, young Danny was obsessed with the space race and he insisted that someday he had to go to the moon. To encourage the dream, his mom ordered shuttle plan wallpaper from the States and helped decorate his bedroom with elaborate space vehicle models that hung from the ceiling; his parents encouraged him to read as many books he could on space travel. The astronauts were his heroes and he could recite by heart the names of those on several missions, and when the Challenger exploded he felt it personally. On that day, Dee and Danny were outside for recess when a teacher ran out to announce the tragedy. They wept then and again when that night the family together watched the news footage over and over and over.

Years later their mom was making dinner while Danny and Dee finished homework at the dining table. Danny looked up from his math, and asked, "I'll never be an astronaut will I, Mom?"

She was gentle. "No, son, you probably won't." Then she tried to redirect him to the many other dreams a boy with humour and kindness might successfully achieve. Dee remembers her mom's compassion, but his impossible dream exhaled with a heavy sigh.

▓

After the city's fortieth murder occurred metres from the safety of my womb room, I first worried about Leah's safety. Then I wondered about him, the man who had died so violently. When I looked him up I found an obituary that read in part:

> HAMER, *Daniel Charles. December 15, 1975–October 8, 2011. It is with deep sorrow that we announce Heaven has called our "Danny" home. Born Nathan Isbister, December of 1975, Daniel became part of the Hamer family in July of 1977. Daniel lived life to the fullest but always on his own terms. Despite years of battling addictions he touched the lives of everyone he met. His mischievous grin and infectious laugh were a beacon in the dark for those that knew him. On October 8, 2011, in Edmonton, Alberta, Daniel could battle his demons no longer. God saw that he was tired and called him to his eternal rest...Also mourning his passing are friends and family too numerous to mention. Earth has lost a hurting soul but heaven has gained an angel.*

There was a list of his family members who mourned him, and so I looked up one of his sisters on Facebook. Her profile picture was one of a smiling preschooler who looked a little like Alistair. I messaged her the story of the book and of the close proximity of my cousin's house. I then asked:

CARISSA: This, I understand, is an odd request, and I understand if it's too painful to talk about Daniel. However, the more research I did into his background the more I hoped I could better know him through his family. I feel that the book would benefit from Daniel's story and from your family's story. It's not clear whether he lived in Alberta Avenue. However, so many of those who fall victim to crime here are those who have been caught in the terrible vortex that is addiction. Would you be willing to talk to me about Daniel's life?

DEE: I would be more than happy to talk to you about my brother. He was my first and best friend and I've missed him every moment since he left us. Feel free to call me.

Over the phone a few days later, Dee was eager to talk. "Danny did everything one hundred and fifty percent or nothing, so that when he ate, he ate to excess, when he laughed, he laughed from his toes," she told me. "Even when he smiled, every inch of his body was smiling and everyone around him felt lighter." The two were inseparable and as they grew he learned by touching the stove, she learned by watching him.

In grade nine, three of his best friends committed suicide. As Dee found solace in youth group and the Good Book, Danny fought the strict religiosity of his parents. He moved out at fifteen, retreated to alcohol in earnest, then dropped out of high school in grade eleven. He was charged with stealing a chocolate bar when he was fourteen and that half year in juvie would be the foundation for the next twenty years' cycling back and forth from jail to unemployment to odd jobs and back to jail. He completed his GED and apprenticed as a carpet layer. Eventually he passed his driver's exam and for a while enjoyed doing floral deliveries until he disappeared to use again and that boss, while she cried with Dee, felt there was nothing else to do but fire him. She had had a son who was an addict and felt she understood Danny. "He is the hardest worker I've ever had," the boss told Dee. "If he could just give me another reason to take a chance on him."

He never quit trying to quit. Over the years Dee paid for rehab at least six times, but he just couldn't get through Step Five. "I think that's the one where you admit to God and others how you've wronged them. I remember him trying; he once called me from jail in Lethbridge to tell me that he had stolen jewellery from me. But, we never could talk about some things."

For a short time he lived across from her Calgary home, in a basement suite and one night she saw a wild party illuminated by every light in his place. It looked like it could go on for days yet he had to work the next morning and there was no way she was going to let him miss work again. She walked across the street and into the unit. Inside, guys and girls were in various stages of intoxication as her brother lay passed out on his second-hand couch in the centre of it all. With her nightie and long hair, she looked like a Mennonite girl in the middle of a biker party. "Everybody out!" she screamed, pointing to the door. "Out."

A huge guy in leather stood straight and towered above her. "Aren't you scared of me?" he asked.

"Get out," she shouted again, terrified that Dan would be hurt or perhaps worse, that he would be fired from another job.

Years later and again late at night, she was roused from bed by knocking at the front door. Dan's drug dealers introduced themselves with the simple wave of the barrel of a gun. She was to come with them and at gunpoint they drove her to an ATM where she cleared Danny's drug debt while her stomach waved with stress contractions. Later she learned Dan had been inside the car behind her kidnappers. He had brought them to her and he had watched without intervention as they took her away.

"Addiction does that. Had you met him sober you would never guess what he was when he was using," Dee said. "He was diametrically opposed, like Jekyll and Hyde. I know he wouldn't have hurt me when he was sober but I can't say that so confidently about when he was using."

Even that knowledge did not stop her from responding to his calls. After she married, her husband would help too and they would often go downtown together to pick Danny up and bring him home to detox. His legs reeked from street rot: "He had these terrible sores from the crack all over his body. It hurt me so bad to see him doing this over and over," she said. "I can see now that it came to a point where my obsession with fixing him was as strong as his obsession to use. Him struggling with addiction and me struggling to make him better," said Dee. "If you wanted a poster child for addiction, it was my brother. If you needed a poster child for enabling, it was me."

When her son was born, everything changed. She knew she couldn't have two babies. "I finally just had to say, 'I didn't break you, and I can't fix you, Dan.'" This conversation still haunts her. "While I know I took on a role and was equally sick, if I had gotten healthier sooner maybe he would have gotten healthier. If I demanded more from him, drawn clearer boundaries. If I had said no to him even one time about paying his drug debt or about driving him downtown, would things be different?"

Dee never stopped believing Dan would get better. However, looking back she knew he was spiralling. When he died, he had meth in his system. He promised he would never do meth.

‖‖

Dee learned of her brother's death over the phone with her mom. The police had identified him by his tattoos and despite that their family had requested his name not be released to the media, it was threaded throughout his network's social media feeds. The boy who was always the last in the bath and the first to laugh, the boy who had cried at the death of astronauts and traded his Bible for candy, the boy who had played baseball all day and had never been able to explain his heritage—his huge body would be cremated and the remains fit in a small urn on Dee's mantle in her Calgary home. It sat there until a friend said, "Did you know you can send ashes to space?"

That night she stayed up late searching the Internet and found a company who, for a thousand dollars, would launch remains beyond the earth's atmosphere. When she contacted Celestis Memorial Spaceflights, they instructed her to ship them a hand-lotion sized bottle of ashes. The funeral home transferred Dan's remains into the bottle and Dee packed the ashes according to Canada Post's instructions. When she arrived at the post office, she told the bored worker that Dan was in the box; the worker shrugged okay.

"Have a good trip!" she said, tapping the box. In New Mexico, the company transferred Dan's remains to a small flat battery with his name inscribed on the side. Then they attached the battery to the head of a rocket. Dee travelled to New Mexico where she met the families of the others travelling with Dan: a Hollywood movie star from the 1960s, Argentina's first female pilot, science teachers and housewives and students were to join him in space.

Before the launch the families stood outside in the humid air for a short memorial service. It was so different from the funeral held four days after Dan died when Dee was still bubble-wrapped in shock. A year and a half later Dee still felt raw, but she was ready to say this goodbye as everyone held their breath on countdown: three, two, one. They watched the rocket rise until a voice broke through the radio static: "We have reached space." The families dissolved in shrieks and tears and laughter. "We've done it," Dee thought. Out loud she said, "Well there you go, Dan. There you go." Looking up she knew that he was sober, blowing raspberries at her with a grin that said, *Now, look who made it to space.*

5

Hell Is Other People

A DECADE AGO our back alley was dotted with shelled
sentries: rusted Buicks and sheds shrunken by fire. Many of the fence
posts leaned like wind-swept trees shading pavement cracks filled
with the deflated balloons of last night's trade of sex for money. These
days most of the cars have been towed and some of the sheds replaced
with modest garages. Yet despite the slowly evolving upgrades, it's an
alley where people still put out old furniture that, unless it's a stained
mattress, will be scooped up by industrious DIYers within the week.
Bottles often sit out separate from the trash, put out in a friendly way
like a tithe for pickup by the shuffling men pushing grocery carts whose
squeaking wheels announce their approach from a block away.

It's an alley where dust rises from bumping cars and is trampled back
down by the feet of bottle pickers and school kids. It's an alley that still
has grace for my overflowing compost pile and wild gardens and I like to
think my cheery red garage door makes the stinking heap of composting
veggies appear quaint and shabby chic. My garage is set directly across
the alley from my neighbour, Siena's, garage. Now that she and her
husband no longer drive, it's her middle-aged son's car that is housed
there; he lives in their basement and silently helps around the yard and

house. His mother's garden was once huge and tidy; however it too has *truly* begun to look shabby chic with a tiny plot of pole beans struggling up among the chickweed battling for space with the self-seeding arugula. One morning she saw me tending my butternut squash plant that sprouted from the end of a skinny raised bed Mat had built. Walking carefully across the broken pavement in her compression stockings and podiatrist-approved shoes, she waved with a closed fist.

"Plant these now," she said in broken English, "and you will have arugula forever."

"Thank you!" I said. "Look at how many flowers I'm getting on this mammoth plant. But no squash ever grow."

"Ah, let me show you," and she plucked one of the male flowers off the spiny plant. Her thick hands gently opened the lips of the female flower and into its mouth the male's central stack went. "Voila!" she said, with passion enough for all of us. "Now, take this inside," she said as she handed me the used up male. "Dip it in whipped egg, dust it with flour and fry it on both sides. You can eat it like a pancake. Or stuff it like manicotti with ricotta cheese and arugula and salt, then pour a marinara sauce over top. It is so delicious. So delicious. Never waste the male flowers!"

She was at her back fence when she shouted, "And always pick them in the mornings, yeah?"

Siena moved into her solid brick bungalow four decades ago after arriving with her husband and Italian vocabulary. In the first few years they planted three skinny apple trees and she gave birth and nursed three kids; two have since moved to the suburbs but return for her babysitting. Her husband owned a shoe repair business on 118th Avenue for years until his lungs got bad and his body weakened so that he could no longer pull his oxygen machine around the small shop. In time, they cut down the apple trees, one, two, then three, because even with their son's help they could not keep up with the windfall, and besides their garden was beginning to struggle for sunshine.

For the first thirty-five years that they lived in their home their neighbours to the south changed often. The house was set far back on the lot and from the alley it looked like a garage. Between them, a short wooden fence slowly rotted.

When a developer bought the vacant lot, Siena was excited that finally there might be some stability next door. As the bulldozers moved rock and soil around, the fence and half of Siena's sidewalk went with it. She mourned. Much of the cement that spread around her house was there thanks to her Italian kinsmen who had come to Canada with masonry skills and set up shop doing what they did best in the old country. Their work in these communities is everywhere still. Selling their services door-to-door, they were masters of thick concrete slabs and stairs and walls and hell, if it could be built with cement, they built it. While they built the sidewalk strong enough to withstand the bumping stems of chickweed and dandelion, it was defenceless against the teeth of a front-end loader hastily driven and due back at the rental place in two hours.

After a year of hearing it from Siena in both ears the builder agreed to pay for a new sidewalk. New owners moved in and brought in their beds and couches and chairs then appeared happy to stay inside. The only reason I know they go out is because their car has left tire imprints in the field of quack grass that grows like a well-fertilized wheat field.

As one can imagine, Siena wants her fence; the culmination of her hopes and dreams for the property to the south is that she not have to see it as she tends her garden. After years of apathy balanced with years of anarchy, these new homeowners offered hope.

"I can't get them to even talk about building a fence," she told me morosely as she set out on one of her daily, post-dinner walks around the block. Siena's neighbours' neighbour, who lives where the garbage heap once slouched, wants to build a fence too but they have the same problem: Wheat-field neighbours are out of cash.

"There's a new grant, Siena," I told her. "The city will match up to one thousand dollars of any exterior project that improves the look of your property. We submitted the receipts for painting the stucco on our house and a cheque came in two weeks. Forget the neighbour! You can just have the city pay Wheat-field neighbour's half!"

"But this is what they want," Siena shook her head. "They want a new fence that is free."

"But what do you want?"

"A fence."

"So just build it," I said.

"But that is what she wants—a free fence."

▥

Thankfully, our neighbour Laura was in favour of building and splitting the cost of a new fence. When we had bought the house our building inspector made a number of clear notes including "fence needs replacing". However, we eked out almost another decade from the rotting boards, then Laura's dog and our children realized they could literally push through. When it came time to fell the leaning boundary, it took one solid heave-ho.

Demolishing the fence was one thing; building a new one was another. Mat and I are wing-it people, meaning we start a project after much thought, but against the advice of many professionals we do little planning. The den on our main floor once was a bedroom with brown shag rug that the dog had been quite sick on from both ends. It had a fan that when rotating shook like our unsecured washing machine. We had spent two years thinking that we should open the room up by widening the single door into a double arch and after two years talking, one Saturday we spent the day cleaning so the floors were washed, windows streak-free and dishes in the cupboards. However when we called our friends to come over and enjoy the clean digs, no one was around. So Mat got out his crowbar and ripped out the drywall that was pasted over hundred-year-old lathe and plaster. He pulled up the nasty rug and I started chipping away the plaster on the red brick chimney at the centre of the house. Dust was everywhere and our project was on.

This method of renovation works for us but Laura, understandably, wanted a plan. We discussed what it would look like: Laura relied on Mat because she did not know what their four hands could legitimately construct and Mat waffled on the design because he prefers to play it by ear.

When Laura went away to Malta for a wedding, talk turned to action. A weekend window had opened up in our calendar and Mat figured that this was the time to take the entire fence down and in a day, it was out and piled high on another neighbour trailer which is always available to do dump runs for the small price of a bottle of whiskey.

Once the fence was out we waited for the post-hole digger, a guy Laura sourced from an Internet buy-sell site. He had references and gave us his licence number in exchange for our deposit, but took his time putting the posts in. In the meantime, Laura's dog sitter was silently freaking out about Seamus the dog who now had no fence or gate so had to be leashed every time he went out in the yard. We did not notice Seamus' unfortunate reality until Laura got back and Mat got a curt text: "my dog's been tied up the entire time I've been away because of this fence."

Relations relaxed as the fence, which included horizontal boards and a wrought iron neighbour gate to replace the old wood one, got built. Neighbours who have lived here longer than I recount that the entire block of back yards were once connected by neighbour gates. By the end of the summer both yards were again secure and our neighbour gate allowed the kids to explore Laura's yard where they would throw Seamus toys, and eventually, finding the kitchen door open, would help themselves to the contents of her candy jar. Laura actively encouraged this by refilling the jar and allowing the visits to include chats about school and exploration of the three bedrooms upstairs that once housed a family of twelve.

Having bought the house from a couple who moved to a small town to raise a family, Laura was excited about living close enough to ride her bike to her work downtown as a director in a small non-profit organization. She frequently travelled, sometimes for fun, other times for the Red Cross. Her stories of responding to the ebola crisis in Sierra Leone managed to hold even the kids' attention one evening as she shared the contents of her Christmas Craft Beer Advent Calendar. When she was not away, she would regularly get to our front sidewalk's snow first with her shovel.

Laura adopted her dog Seamus from a rescue organization about the same time she bought the house, and despite being the size of a small pony, he constantly skittered and shied away from the sounds of our neighbourhood: Loud motorbikes, AC/DC in the open-air football stadium ten blocks south, fireworks from the fairgrounds ten blocks east, thunder from the towering cumulus clouds that prompted tornado warnings. While poor Seamus would cower in fear, he rarely barked.

One small design flaw in our fence allowed for any sized dog to slip under the fence and often Seamus popped over to our yard to sniff for chicken bones and misplaced peanut butter cookies. One afternoon, he found Lily's half-eaten carrot, then gently picked it up and carried it to his bed to sleep sweetly with it all night.

As we celebrated the completion of our new fence with cold beer, Laura jokingly said, "I'm glad we can still talk after a project like this." We were moving on to our next joint project, discussing how our landscaping could complement the fence and reduce the grass on her side and I agreed with her, thankful we had a relationship that could be honest *and* kind.

Neighbour relationships are of an unusual type, while perhaps not as emotionally close as colleagues, neighbours know far more intimate details. Our neighbours know that we drive our van instead of take the bikes to school; that I am most impatient when we are trying to leave the house or finish my morning coffee without interruption; that our kids stay up well beyond the bedtimes of most other kids; that we sleep in and practise our instruments poorly. Mat's caught a glimpse of neighbours having a late-night glass of milk in the nude. Or, when I had folks from down the block over for the first time, they said, "It's a lovely garden from this vantage point too." They pointed to a window two doors down which apparently has a perfect view of our back yard; whether they have seen me in the nude with my glass of milk, I never had the courage to ask.

One Saturday during the spring after our new fence was built, our growing children and their loud, expanding clan of friends strained Laura's patience paper-thin. The kids woke her up in the morning and their noise drifted all day like tidal currents out the front door, out the back door, out the side windows, and into her life.

"I'm sorry about the kids this morning," Mat said. He sat with a friend, drinking a beer under the blooming apple tree. "Did they wake you?"

"I forget just how close we all are," she said wryly. "But I just put my ear plugs in. The thing is, I'd just like the one day I take off work to be a little quieter. I can't even keep my windows open." She had to raise her voice to be heard over the high-pitched sounds of a game that required Ali to provide siren sounds at top volume. The following awkward pause was filled with the sounds of kids squabbling about the correct pitch of an air raid horn.

6

May the Punishment
Fit the Crime

DRIVING HOME from a mid-day summer play at the park, we were a block south of our home when I saw my first hit and run. We were all antsy to cool down in the basement; however, as we turned towards our alley, a steel boat of a car slowed us to a crawl. Boat Driver was going about as slowly as one could without technically being stopped. Perhaps he was consulting his paper map circa 1989 or talking loudly on his phone, conveniently built in to the centre console. Or, perhaps Boat Driver was simply out for a Sunday drive.

Whatever he was doing, it was slowing us down and we had an appointment with *My Little Pony*. As I moved to tap our horn, a man on a bike shot out from the alley. He was riding as though hell threatened to swallow him up. He didn't look back, nor did he look side to side as he neared the road. With one arm holding his bike upright as it bumped over the alley's uneven tarmac, the other arm hugged a fishing rod and tool kit.

His speed was double Boat Driver's while his weight was like a fruit fly's compared to the elephant that was the car. There were no signs that he even attempted to brake and as he hit the rumbling car his slight body bounced into the opposite lane empty of oncoming traffic. The bike lay crooked on its side in the middle of the road, his gear was scattered across the street, and the universe paused for a moment of silence. Then Boat Driver and I opened our doors. Just as frantically Bike Guy struggled to get up. He stood crookedly as we stepped onto the pavement and he reached for the tackle box even as he rubbed his elbow. Then, with the box in hand, he limp-ran away across the street, through some tall Canadian thistle and disappeared behind a crumbling shed. There was no blood as we moved the bike onto the sidewalk and respectfully gathered what he left behind. None of it was from my garage.

IIIII

I almost hit a guy on a bike that next autumn. Rain fell onto icy streets and I was driving slowly when a group of three people meanderingly cycled their way across the road. I stepped on the brakes. The leader had a child's trailer attached to his mountain bike and it was full of blue bags stuffed with what I presumed to be bottles. Of the two others who followed him, one woman wore a black hoodie that made her nearly invisible in the dark and another man pulled a plywood trailer stacked with pieces of drywall wrapped in plastic. It teetered dangerously as the group irreverently cut off traffic and an F-150 honked as it slowed its charge.

Lily shouted from the back, "Mommy, I just saw a guy with a bike pulling a bunch of stuff he stole."

"The bottle depot's back there, honey. I think he was carrying bags of bottles."

"No, those were filled with kids' toys," she insisted.

"I'm pretty sure they were bottle collectors. And for their job they usually need a way to transport the bottles they get to the bottle depot. See, the depot is there." It was actually in the opposite direction to where the bikes were headed.

"No, he had toys in there."

"Okay, maybe."

"He stole them." She was sure. "He should go to jail!"

"Jail? You think he should go to jail for stealing toys?" She had no idea that jail wasn't like some two-minute timeout. "Maybe there's some other punishment."

"Nope. Jail," she said.

I tried a different approach. "So if a man steals something..."

"Like Poodley," Lily interrupted with the name of her favourite stuffy.

"So the man steals Poodley, what could he do to make up for that instead of jail?"

"See a judge?" Lily asked. I was surprised that the six-year-old even knew the word.

"Okay, so maybe the judge could ask him why he stole Poodley. Maybe the judge would tell him to talk to you about it and you'd tell him how you cried for three nights because you didn't have her. Then, he'd hear how bad you felt and he'd feel so bad that he would return Poodley and say sorry. Would that be enough punishment?"

"Yeah," she paused. "People sometimes steal stuff because they're really sad, right?" Lily said, "If he was sad, I'd tell him he could keep the Poodley for nine days." God, I loved her.

I wanted to pursue the idea of justice, so offered a less personal scenario. "What if a kid stole some pizzas from the fun lunch at school?"

"Yeah, like he was really hungry."

"Should he get into trouble then?"

"No, I'd give him some of my money for pizza," Lily offered. "Or maybe I'd just give him some of my pizza,"

"What if the kid stole the pizza because he had four already and just wanted another? Would you think differently?" I asked.

She shrugged, "I'd give him more money to buy more pizzas then."

She was struggling to understand the difference between the thefts so I told a Sunday school story that I hadn't thought of for many years:

Once there was a very rich man who had many, many animals and servants and gold and houses. He lived next to a very poor man who owned one lamb that he was preparing to sell at the market so he could make money to feed

his own family. The rich man was to hold a party. The chef asked him what
he would like him to prepare and the rich man ordered lamb: a specific lamb,
he wanted the poor man's lamb. So, the chef went over to the poor man's
home and took the lamb while the family slept. He served the lamb to the
rich man's guests.

When the poor man discovered that his lamb was gone, he cried. When
he discovered who had taken it, he told the rich man, "You must pay me for
that lamb." But the rich man refused to pay.

Lily wailed from the back. "That's not fair! But he had so many!"

Her horror rose as literal steam on the windows and I flipped on the defrost. "If you were a judge, what would you do to make it right?"

"I'd take all the rich man's animals away but leave him with just two. Then he could get milk and stuff." She was quiet, and then said: "No, I think I'd take half his animals away and give them to the poor man." It was not quite a restorative solution, but one that I could get one hundred percent behind.

7

The Case of the
Missing Hundred Bucks

TAYLOR WAS EIGHT YEARS OLD when I met him at the Ship Park, behind the Alberta Avenue Community League, and he was one of those kids who found the gravitational pull of adults in the park to be far stronger than the call of his peers playing tag. When he did play it was gently, with the littlest kids.

My first born, Madi, was a small two when she first chased him and predictably fell on the rubberized playground mat. "Are you okay?" he asked in a sing-song voice as he picked her up. "I'm sorry I was going so fast!" He wiped off the crumbs of rubber imprinted on her knee, then distracted her by falling over as though she had kicked him.

"Ughh-awwww," he play-acted a sore shin, which made her laugh so hard that she lost complete control of her drool.

The summer we met him turned into fall and he began to come around to the house to visit. At first he came with a pretense like raking leaves or shovelling the walk. However, soon he simply came to visit a pregnant adult woman and her toddler child. When I asked his mom, Tanya, if it was okay, she said, "Of course. It's quieter over there."

Taylor was the fourth in a family of nine children and they lived across the street and half a block up from us in a two-bedroom house with a basement where the three oldest boys found some privacy. His dad worked in building maintenance while his mom home-schooled the kids.

Madi began to notice his stretches of absence, days and occasionally weeks, where he wouldn't come to play. "Where's Taylor?"

"He's in a place where he can eat as much Jell-O as he wants!" I told her, then immediately regretted it.

"Can I go too?"

We visited him once at the children's hospital where there was colour and light and lots of friendly nurses in cheery garb. When we came into the room, Taylor beamed and gave us an exuberant tour of the halls to the hallowed Jell-O fridge. In his room, the bench-like bed that his mom, and sometimes dad, collapsed on most nights was prepped with a pillow for another uncomfortable night.

Their nightmare had begun the morning of Taylor's seventh birthday. His buzzing energy was amplified by the fact that this was the one day in the year where the big family celebrated and focused on just him. Tanya told him to get clean. She heard the shower run, then the high squeaking of slipping feet and a dull thud as his light frame collapsed in the bath with kidney failure. He would survive the next year with hours of dialysis until a donor was found.

The family decided to rent out the home they owned outside the city and move into the most affordable neighbourhood in Edmonton, Alberta Avenue. In the eight-hundred-square-foot home, the youngest slept with his parents while Taylor and his two middle siblings shared the front bedroom. The four youngest kids did their home-school work in the dining room and, in the warm months, on the front porch that looked out to a yard that the family's giant dog had returned to dirt. Sometimes in the evenings, the younger kids' laughter from the porch would be replaced with the sounds of two oldest kids jamming on their acoustic guitars. Tanya trusted her kids, and they wandered with fairly wide boundaries to the 7-Eleven or the bakeries. The bakeries would become a problem for Taylor whose meds began to mess with his metabolism so that he was hungry all the time.

The first time the youngest three kids came to our house they were on
a donation drive. They knocked on the door and patiently held out a
Kleenex box covered in construction paper. When we opened the door,
the five-year-old said, "We're raising money for our church. Do you have
any change?"

Mat did and parted with it. They came by again the next day, still
raising money for their church and did we have any change?

Mat did, but asked, "Do you know what you're raising the money for?"

They shrugged, looked at each other and then at Mat blankly.

"Come back with a letter and I'll donate a little more."

The two youngest came back a couple of days later. "We're collecting
money for church," the four-year-old said, then simply wiggled the box in
front of Mat.

"Did you bring me a letter?"

He shook his head, and then from behind our front yard's lilac bush
came the hissing whisper-shout of Taylor: "Tell him it's for youth group."
That's when we figured it was quite possibly all made up and when we
knew Taylor was surely going to go to business school someday.

The first time I let Taylor enter our house, he rang the doorbell and
when I opened the door he handed me a plastic rose in a melamine vase.
It probably cost a buck at the dollar store down the street, the same store
that sold bongs alongside cleaning supplies and popsicles of all varieties.
I was miserably pregnant, on bed rest, and the eight-year-old had
cheered me.

He chatted at me as he followed me into the living room where I had
set up a bed-rest station on the couch. He told me about the new baby
born in the green house down the street. He told me how the old lady
up the block had gone to the hospital. He told me about his plans for a
lemonade stand in the summer, then asked me if he could shovel the
walk and so I paid him some change for the favour.

The next summer, we saw a lot more of him. He first mowed our front sloping lawn of dandelions, quack grass and those terrible heart-shaped weeds that creep with incredible tenaciousness into the flowerbeds, and successfully navigated the three ant piles. He had an old push mower donated by a neighbour and despite its questionable blade and small operator, we paid him five dollars to do the front and back yards: three hundred square feet of weed-lawn.

When he finished the first time, he hung out in the backyard with Madi, and throwing the grass in the air so that it fell on him, he shouted, "Madi, I'm a pizza!" She scooped grass up too and tossed it on his feet, which were clad in one green and one red Croc.

Sometimes he would bring his younger brothers along to visit, and sometimes he would bring his guinea pig, which would wiggle, twisting and scratching out of the toddler's clutching grip to disappear, one time, under the deck where his recovery required Mat's drill and the removal of no less than seven cedar deck boards.

Just before Madi's third birthday, on the Friday of the first weekend of October, I noticed I was missing one hundred and twenty dollars from the drawer where we kept our monthly cash allotments. I had taken out the twenties a few days before, but left them in a stack at the front of the drawer until I could distribute them into the small files that helped define our budget. When I finally got around to filing the bills I realized we were short twenty dollars in entertainment and still needed fifty for gifts and another fifty for house maintenance. I checked my receipt to confirm I had withdrawn enough money.

"Did you use any cash?" I asked Mat.

"No, why?"

A terrible thought emerged; it had been sitting back there since the summer barbecue where at least seven sets of parents attempted to keep their bearings as food and kids and garbage swirled around us like a rip tide. In the middle of this, my oldest girlfriend handed me a hundred-dollar bill. "What's this for?" I asked.

"I owe you for the groceries you bought for the last freezer meal cook-off we had at Hannah's," Katy said. I remember placing the brown bill on the buffet in the kitchen then immediately got swept away with the arrival of yet more food and kids. Taylor entertained the preschoolers at that party.

Despite my instinct to dismiss the idea—its sheer presence felt like a betrayal—I reflected back on the last two days of people who had visited. Taylor had been the only visitor and in fact, that afternoon Taylor and Madi had played in the office next to the cash drawer.

I spoke my fear out loud to Mat who felt the same way as I: badly, and like it was a possibility. "Call Tanya," Mat said as I had apparently pulled the short straw.

"Hey, Tanya?" We spoke about the cooling weather and new school year.

"Listen, I'm going to say this only because I don't know of any other solution to my problem," I started cryptically, "but I say it only as information for you just in case you've seen some evidence that might help me."

I took a breath. "We're missing a little over two hundred dollars in cash from the house. It disappeared over a couple different times and at first I thought we'd misplaced it. I hate that I'm saying this, but Taylor is the only one I can think of who was around both times. So, if there seems to be a sudden flush of cash...then, I don't know..."

Tanya took a second then said, "I'm so glad you called. Yes, there has been money around here." Taylor had miraculously found eighty dollars under a rock. He had taken his brothers and sister out to the fast food taco place on the Avenue and brought home doughnuts for the family. As I leaned against the counter top facing the backyard, Taylor came into view. He carried a bulging Value Village bag, the large kind they keep for overgrown stuffies and couch cushions. The handles were stretched thin, barely keeping up with the weight of the loot which he mostly dragged up the deck steps.

"Tanya, he's here and he's got a bag full of stuff from Value Village."

She didn't hesitate. "I'm coming over."

She was there in under two minutes, enough time for Taylor to begin his role as Santa Claus to which Madi was held rapt, as much by the singing quality of his voice as the coloured plastic toys with tangled hair that emerged from the bag. "Madi, I got you and Lily some presents."

My heart fell like an anchor attempting to remain moored as he pulled out Barbies and My Little Ponies. He showed me a ring that he had bought for his mom and gave me a pack of cards. He wasn't at all tipped off when his mom, who rarely came over, arrived. He proudly showed her the ring he bought her using stolen money from this very house, and she said firmly, "I see, Taylor. We need to have a chat."

Madi watched TV with her new ponies and dolls lined up attentively, as the adults and Taylor sat in the living room. His mom opened the meeting:

"Taylor, did you steal the money you said that you found under a rock?"

"Mom, no!"

"How did you get this money for Value Village?"

"Mom, I told you. From under a rock." For the next ten minutes, he adamantly denied that he had lied, that he had stolen, that he had ever hurt us.

I believed him on the last count. I knew that that first hundred-dollar bill must have seemed too good to be true. He was always hustling with his mower or his lemonade stands. I also couldn't forget the way the meds made him feel. The dietician at the clinic had started to put her foot down and he was on a strict diet where Tanya had even told me to stop giving him foods with high fat or high sugar. He had been begrudgingly eating hummus with pita at my place. On the sly, however, he made trips to 7-Eleven and the bakery. In fact, one of the ladies at the bakery had beamed at me when I was there with him and the girls. "Are you his mom?" Nope, and I tensed. "Well, he's here every day and he's a delight." These frequent, illicit trips for food needed funding.

I wanted desperately to tell Tanya to forget I had called. It was nothing. We could absorb the loss and, besides, we didn't really know who took it. I knew, however, that that would only embarrass her further. When they left the house, Taylor's face was a red, stoic mask and his mom was as full of apology as I was.

His dad called us later. "Taylor took the money."

I apologized and he said gruffly, "Don't be sorry. Those gifts were guilt presents. He knew he wasn't supposed to take that money."

As we headed up the steep stairs for Madi's bedtime routine that included three glasses of milk, five trips up and down the stairs, and usually a parent falling asleep in her short bed, there was a knock on the door. Tanya stood under the porch light and Taylor stood on the sidewalk.

"Come up here, please, Taylor," she said gently.

His hoodie shook with his head, no.

Mat and I climbed down the steps to stand just a few feet away from our dear young friend. We waited and without a word, Taylor fell face forward on the soaking dandelion hill and cried with the sky. His body heaved great sobs that I matched with similar distress.

"We aren't mad," Mat said. "We just want the truth so we can make it right." Eventually Taylor stood up and muttered. "Sorry," but he couldn't meet our eyes.

"We'll pay you back," Tanya said.

"Please, no," we said. Seeing Taylor's shame had been enough for us, but perhaps not enough consequence for him. I knew to not accept the money was to add to his parents' embarrassment so the next day it was agreed that Taylor had lost the privilege to come into our home, a place that had come to be a stage where the spotlight was mostly on him before an admiring audience. His parents paid us back and Taylor paid them back by shovelling our walks for free that entire winter. And so, we did get to see flashes of his black ski jacket in flurries of snow and when he was done, he would wave at the front window where Madi stood with a dozen gifted ponies lined up, half of them having lost their manes as their new owner perfected her scissor skills. Madi would wave back then watch our friend move on to another paying gig.

8

Friend Stalking

MOM AND I WERE OUTSIDE my house looking at the awful condition of the stucco: 1960s pebble dash that is a layer of tan brown cement spotted with shattered glass bits like doughnut sprinkles. As we discussed solutions to my home's slumping skin, a woman, her belly taut with a child, came into view. She stopped to breathe and as one does with very pregnant women, we asked her for details about the baby and herself. Having recently moved to the neighbourhood from Calgary, she had started a new job with the government. Now very overdue, she walked in the hopes of jostling this first baby out and behind the frames of her stark white glasses, her eyes were tired.

Her name was Drea, short for Andrea, and we didn't meet again until three years later in the newly opened Eastwood Health Clinic, built to replace the mould-filled health unit on 118th Avenue across from the Drive-In Burger Baron. The public health nurses who worked there were our school nurses, community dieticians, and nurse practitioners. It's where every baby in the neighbourhood visits from the age of two months to two years and there have their heads measured, bodies weighed, then their unsuspecting arms or thighs pinched and poked by needles.

On the day I met Drea again, the signs of spring poked through the melting snow as I waited for Alistair's first set of shots. A woman with a beautiful sling—a black damask pattern on baby blue background—emerged from the back and her son had already settled with her breast in his mouth while a blonde daughter waited, eyeing Lily shyly.

"Your sling, I love it," I said.

"Yeah, it has saved me many insane afternoons," she laughed. So began the relaxed chatter than comes when two women of similar age, education levels, culture, and life stage meet without the pulling pressures of work. Maternity leaves have a way of slowing time down and we were both into the second phase of our leaves where our schedules and homes had acclimatized to the babies and our older children were beginning to drive us bonkers with their need for socialization. The first few weeks of infancy out of the way, our own exhaustion had melted into feelings of friendship starvation.

I had met another girlfriend at the volunteer-driven Carrot Coffeehouse's Friday Babes in Arms group in this phase of maternity leave who joked that she had become a friend stalker. Strapping her four-month daughter into the stroller Trish would march about the neighbourhood in search of poor souls standing about. She was new to the city without extended family close by, so she visited the coffee shops, the convenience stores, the parks, always scanning for potential friends. When she spotted a target, she would laugh loudly, catch people's eye, then say something unexpected, preferably about her daughter, so they felt compelled to engage.

||||

After a short pause and as I shifted Ali over to the other breast, she said, "Do you live on the street south of the bakery?" I nodded. She said, "I think we met when I was really pregnant with my daughter."

"Was I with my mom? On the front sidewalk?"

"Yeah, you were thinking of renovating and I was trying to walk a baby out."

"I can't believe we've lived a block from each other all this time and not run into each other since then," I said.

"It's been hard to connect," she said. "We've been thinking of moving away closer to where my husband works."

Feeling a sudden urge to convince her to stay, I took a chance and invited her to the local gymnastics club the next Friday morning. It was preschool drop-in day and the boot room's metal shelves were full of dozens of pairs of runners and gumboots. Tucked between 118th Avenue and a major arterial road, in the converted warehouse kids crawled, ran, and twirled around on the expansive mats. They balanced on the beams, jumped on the trampoline, and mostly left the double hoops alone because there weren't many supervising adults willing to actively lift them up and spot them.

As Trish, Drea and I left the gym, like a guy who flings his arm around the back seat of his first-date's movie seat, I said, "If you ladies have nothing else to do, we can go back to my place. I'll make something easy."

That afternoon I made black bean soup for the adults while the children managed with soda crackers, apple slices, cheese strings, and milk. My childhood friend and old college roommate, Katy, dropped by as she was in the neighbourhood also looking for friends.

"Wine?" I asked around four.

At about five, I pulled out some nachos and salsa and at six we realized we had visited until dinner with the odd pause to break up a fight or apply a bandage.

That day began a tradition that would last most of the next eight months of maternity leave. Fridays we would gather. Other friends would often join us: Hannah and Naomi and their three kids each. We would parent as little as possible, shouting encouragement or advice from the picnic blanket at the park, or table in the backyard. We would frequently set up camp all day in the museum and only a couple times did the voice of security come over the speaker system in the dinosaur room to say, "Please get off the specimens."

These were days filled with politics and spirituality, education and debate—made even more hilarious in the presence of compassionate women with wonky hormones wielding a bunch of poorly sourced facts. In the midst of the crazy, Drea's phone's meditation bell would chime—*dong*—every half hour reminding her to take a centering breath. Together we searched for—and frequently lost—balance.

|||||

The last evening, Drea, Trish, and I were all together we were at Drea's place and I drank kombucha green tea while Drea sipped her homemade juice from a straw. Her mouth and throat were dry and when she wasn't talking her breath rasped like trees waving rough against the window. Trish and I regaled her with stories of work, and she laughed at us while shifting uncomfortably on the couch. The cancer in her liver had grown, despite a trip to Mexico, drastic chemo, estrogen pills, juicing and early morning meditation.

Her children had slept over at our houses on alternate weekend nights while she travelled for treatment and we told her how they had helped set up Ali's spy party for his fifth birthday, how they had hiked kilometres in the snow, how they had missed her. As she sipped her steady diet of juice filled with local kale and organic veggies, Trish and I ate what we found in the fridge, because this was how it had always been the last four years. Eat what you want, drink what you want, just bring yourself.

At her memorial—celebration—(whatever these things are called where all I wanted to do was rip out my hair and tear my clothes and scream that life was unfair and cancer fucking sucked), Trish and I were given the microphone. We spoke of our meeting, of mat-leave-Fridays, of Drea's bottomless snack purse, of our monthly craft nights where we spray painted crappy furniture and painted murals. We remembered some of our rowdiest wine clubs that Drea hosted and which expanded the friend circle far wider than moms with young kids.

We remembered our family camping trips too. The baby boys were two when our families walked five kilometres in to a campsite at Elk Island National Park with seven children under seven all enthralled by the trail of squashed frogs which led us to a field where bison shat and ate. That night in the middle of a bison latrine, Drea calmed the kids down by drawing pictures on their backs: rain and rainbows, sunshine and butterflies.

Once the kids were in bed, the adults circled the fire and Drea sang some pop song loudly, which seemed to bring out the fireflies. As we marvelled at the lights that filled the field, we noticed thick fog that rolled off the nearby swamp water. Inside the mist, three hulking bison walked as silently as ghosts and then, without warning, Drea ran into the fog straight towards them. Even though our hands in front of our faces were invisible, we ran after her into the dark.

▥

The night of the memorial, Drea's family, friends and neighbours danced in the small living room in the house of Gillian, Drea's dear friend. It was a century old two-storey within stumbling radius of my home. That night the walls were pasted with photos of Drea as a ballet dancer, Drea as mom, Drea as adventure hiker, Drea as party girl, Drea as sister, Drea as daughter, Drea as friend, Drea as wife. Dollar-store butterflies on wires decorated the entryway and staircase, they hung from lights and stood tall pillared in plant pots, and as the crowd of grieving friends' dancing feet shook the floor, the butterflies on their thin wires moved in remembrance too.

9

Billian's Safe House

I HEARD ABOUT GILLIAN before I met her. Drea's good friend lived a few blocks east of us and she was renowned for her perpetual motion, humour, and animal activism. In the early days of our friendship, Drea sometimes worried about Gillian because she had offered the empty guest room in her house to a neighbour who had been kicked out of his rooming house. "I mean, it's a nice thing, right?" Drea said to me. "The guy can't be bad—he saves feral cats!"

Bill saved cats well before his friendship with Gillian started. The first set of kittens he took in was brought to his attention by a desperate mewing from the blackened garage that slumped behind his six-suite rooming house. Someone had failed to fully burn the building down and while no one was charged, there were rumours another tenant had tossed the match. Approaching the structure, Bill spotted three noses poking out from under the freshly cut piece of plywood his landlord hung to ensure no further mischief would happen. Bill put down the food and water he had carried and pulled on the plywood until it popped from its soft wood moorings. The kittens mewed in relief as they drank the water and then followed Bill to the front of his home where he set them up comfortably under the wooden stairs.

These three kittens were the product of a union between two abandoned cats as they waited patiently for the return of their owners. Bill had noticed the cats' human family packing up the moving truck and the next day drove away with everything they owned except for their four feline pets lounging on the front porch. After three days watching from his suite, Bill took action. He set up a feeding station under his porch steps and the pack's habits began to change. Drawn under the stairs for food, they stayed and as none of them were spayed or neutered, they procreated.

The first litter was born in the garage just two blocks west of our home, sheltered and close to mama's sugar daddy Bill. Bill was not technically allowed cats in the house, but the other tenants technically weren't allowed to do or deal drugs. When the kittens got old enough to be separated from their mother, he smuggled them up to his single room, which contained a hot plate, fridge, and space for a bed, then set about domesticating them. Even if the mother is a domestic cat, if kittens grow up without human contact they become feral. They don't tolerate being touched; they scavenge for food, and generally face an untimely death from frostbite, dehydration, or starvation. Others die horribly either caught in the engines of cars that start without warning after the cats warm themselves on the block heater, picked up by birds or captured and (so goes the rumour) used as bait for dog fight rings. Feral cats die in a myriad of ways and Bill couldn't bear the thought, so he petted the kittens and litter trained them and, when he deemed them ready for a new home, put out a homemade cardboard sign on his front lawn: *Free kittens*.

The street on which Bill lived in Alberta Avenue was a major thoroughfare for elementary school kids tromping to school, and invariably those who could read would stop and beg to take a kitten home. He had one rule: they needed a note from a parent.

The family of four cats weren't the only felines abandoned that year, a time of booming oil business. Up and down the street, people moved in and out nearly as fast as a drive-thru order can be turned around and in the shuffle, as the rental market became increasingly resistant to pets of any kind, people left their animals.

The housing market was a rising fever and everyone was delirious. Owners like us were spending-mad with new-found equity wealth. Many renters, however, found themselves at the short end of an economic boom where new landlords came and went and almost always raised the rent and tightened conditions. The boom meant that many homes in Alberta Avenue, which had a rental rate of over seventy per cent, changed owners. It was true of even Bill's shitty rooming house which sold for $95,000, then again a few months later for $130,000.

As the only non-drug user tenant in his house, Bill managed to retain a room until the last couple bought it and thought they would like to live in it themselves. Even then, he didn't have to move far as one of his former landlords still owned the run-down rooming house next door. Resettled twenty feet north, his cat rescue operation continued. It was in front of this house that Bill met Gillian. She lived across the street and had a bad feeling about the *Free kittens* sign. She had been watching the cardboard sign go up and down over the past year and had watched the children stop and exclaim, and talk to the broad, grey-haired man who walked stiffly with a slight limp that favoured his right side. With the drug house as backdrop she determined to check in with the man herself.

‖‖‖‖

Gillian told me the story when I finally met her and Bill in the living room of her, or their, house. "You have free kittens?" she had asked Bill.

"Yes, I do. Would you like one?" Bill said.

"I'd like to see one, yes," Gillian said. "I'd like to see a few, even."

He led her up the wood stairs, down a hallway and to his room that had an attached bathroom. She wondered if he lived on anything beyond macaroni, margarine and bread.

Just as he promised, there were kittens and eight adults cats that he cared for in the neighbourhood, from a shelter underneath his front steps.

"Do they stay outside in the winter?" she asked of the feral cats.

Bill knew that bylaw officers could shut the house down if the cats all lived with him so he resigned himself to regularly visiting the Front Step Shelter and replacing the frozen water in the dish with warm. "Abandoned domestics don't know to eat snow and they must have water," he told her.

"I think you need a plan," said Gillian. "You won't solve the issue if you simply keep domesticating kittens and giving them away."

"I have no money to neuter any of them," he said.

"Well, I have money." Then Gillian came up with a deal where she would provide cash and transportation for the cats to be neutered and she agreed that none of the cats in their care would be put down.

While his home may have been a safe home for cats, it wasn't getting much safer for Bill. He had been injured at work twenty years before and had never been able to go back to his trade. Bill refused to go on government disability because he felt he could "work a little bit". That work, however, rarely materialized. Occasionally, he had house-sat other properties for his landlord that helped stretch his measly monthly income to include cat food. For a time, he managed his own rooming house, but he quit that when the other tenants refused to stop putting the heat up to thirty degrees. Every night he would turn the heat down before bed and every night the partying tenants would turn it up until one night he had turned the heat down only to be awakened a little later by a tenant outside his door complaining about the cold. He decided he was tired of the conflict and went back to being a tenant where one night he escaped a house fire. Another night he slept poorly as the two brothers who rented the upstairs suite punched and stabbed one another.

It wasn't ideal, but it was a roof over his head and he felt thankful that he could afford the roof and flush toilet; then his landlord sold the place and shortly thereafter the new owner knocked on his door. Bill invited the big man in and the man said, "You've got to leave. See, I'm going to do a bunch of renos and so you can't live here anymore."

"Sure, I can do that," he nodded agreeably. "You'll need to give me three months."

"No, you're not understanding me. You need to leave now."

"Well, I need to find another place."

The tall man stood up and breathed down at him. "You're not hearing me. Get the fuck out of my place."

Bill would stay until about the end of the month, but it became rather impossible to stay any longer when the New Landlord Guy ratcheted down the heat to bare minimum and turned the power off. It was winter and becoming increasingly difficult for Bill to look after the two cats who lived with him (but never tolerated being touched). Gillian was preparing to head to Australia for doctoral research and Bill had agreed to feed and water her four cats. When she heard about the eviction, she said, "Bill, why don't you house sit for me? You need a place to stay and I need a house sitter."

Bill moved into her guest room. He stayed for three months and when she returned, she suggested he just stay where he had settled. Gillian told me that in his careful way, he moved around the house tidying, cooking, feeding cats and people. The two unlikely roommates played crib together and listened to 1930s jazz and modern opera that hummed from her grandma's record player.

At Gillian's they continued caring for, trapping and neutering cats but they had to do it a little more carefully because Gillian's neighbours had a love-hate relationship with their project. Many of the neighbours couldn't be bothered with the feral cats and they argued that Gillian and Bill were luring them in by feeding them. However, with the certainty of sunrise when an abandoned kitten litter was found or aggressive magpies were seen pecking the unprotected animals, Team Bill/ian's house was where the neighbours went for help.

Thanks to their work, every spring there were fewer and fewer free-ranging cats to manage on the street until one year there was only one more cat to catch. Angel was black with all white paws. A Chinese neighbour had told Bill that this kind of cat was called "walking on snow" and, according to her tradition, would bring good luck. Angel more literally had good luck with many tomcats and she brought new life to many kittens. Averaging two litters a year, every time Gillian and Bill trapped her, she would be either pregnant or nursing and there was a small window of opportunity to spay this lovely creature. Finally, on a fall day in a vacant lot down the alley, Gillian and Bill trapped Angel at a time when she could be spayed and they invited her to live with them. Angel agreed that she might try it, just for the winter. In the years Bill knew her as a street cat, she was a walking skeleton but as the months wore on at Gillian's, she got fat, so fat that even her paws bulged and just as Gillian and Bill began to worry about her cardiovascular system, she disappeared the first summer in a decade that the block didn't have a feral cat problem.

10

This Neighbourhood Does Not Tolerate Crappy Infill

IN MY NEIGHBOURHOOD sometimes I set out for the two-block stroll to the bakery and halfway there stand startled by a gaping hole in a lot that I swear just yesterday had a house. Like, it was just there and had been for a hundred years. In fact, for the past ten years I had walked by it every day and now I couldn't remember one distinct detail about it. Sometimes I can recall the missing home vaguely: that it was pink or crooked or smelled of cat. At other times, all I can conjure is generic memories of a house with walls and a roof and windows. I find this happens to me a lot these days. The gaps, and what they say about my observation skills, are disorienting.

The houses that fill these gaps are contentious. Builders say it's expensive to do such infill because out on prime farmland and/or wetlands developers can build twenty houses in a row. With infill, one has to buy an expensive lot, and then spend thousands to take the old house down. Next a builder must modify standard house plans to accommodate the various bylaws that govern the site, which may be different from the other neighbourhood they built in last year. Astute builders will then further customize the house to "fit in" to the surrounding block and as they build they pay more because they aren't buying trusses for twenty houses and the electrician's travel time doubles.

Buyers say they want to live in the older communities closer to downtown, but they don't want to live in the seven hundred-square-foot cat house. Because the market in our community is still on the low side, the non-custom infill going up in Alberta Avenue is fairly plain, with standard truss lines and houses framed as simple boxes. The odd builder will add some river rock to the front porch pillars, and in these MLS listings they will tell buyers the home is "New AND Beautiful." Buyers are buying these homes if not for their newness and beauty, then for their price in comparison to any other new house in the city.

In recent days, perhaps because enough people phoned with their opinions about out-dated infill rules and confusing processes, the city started a community consultation process to talk to builders, buyers, and neighbours (a group who are often less strategic than the home builders and far louder than the homebuyers) specifically about infill strategy.

IIIII

At poorly facilitated public consultations where NIMBY Neighbour gets all the mic time, one tends to hear a lot of complaints, but a public consultation never feels complete unless you get a rant on parking. Like most cities in North America, ours has been designed for the car. Wide roads and stretching suburban homes spottily serviced by public transit makes owning a car a virtual must if one can afford it. Alberta Avenue's first homes pre-date the car and some of the roads in our communities are only wide enough for two lanes of traffic and one side of parking, which can make the issue of parking a pivotal conflict.

In fact, many a development permit has lived or died on the city's development committee's table over the issue. I remember one community meeting where neighbours had gathered in the Community League's Lutz Room, a community space that can hold a hundred or so people seated and when I arrived there was standing room only. A city staffer at the front called the meeting to order and behind her stood a tall man with a shock of dark hair who shuffled his notes and straightened the tiny model that represented the poster behind him, a drawing of the new building his company hoped to build on a large block along 95th Street, one of the community's main arteries into downtown.

The block was once populated with war-time bungalows, single-storey homes with cement stairs and a pink stuccoed storefront that housed a bar whose windows advertised all the best abbreviations: "VLTS" and "ATMS" in neon glow dulled by years of layered mud spray from the Number 5 bus. The homes had long been neglected and when the developer bought the stretch of block, he tore them all down. It was a long block that, as it waited for development approvals, was repopulated by resilient maple saplings, nettle and dandelions.

To the uninitiated the development process is like walking into a field of deep fog. The process has a vocabulary of its own. For years when I heard anything about bylaws, permits, re-zoning, or variances, my eyes would lose focus and I would begin thinking about lunch. By the time I finally wrapped my mind around the language, I realized that the process itself, with its applications and consultations, appeals and boards and angry neighbours, was enough to make me quickly lose my appetite.

In the Lutz Room, the developer who shifted uncomfortably in front of me was from a town just outside the city settled during the Cold War and whose streets are named for the birds and trees they displaced. The builder hoped to access provincial and local government money set aside for the creation of more affordable housing.

Affordable housing isn't always subsidized housing; however it has the same reputation. I lived in affordable housing one year in university where the townhouses were simple structures: square and boxy, with a shared field of grass in the back where kids of all ages and colours played soccer late into the fall. Its only difference between my upbringing in a 1970s development full of wide lots and single-family houses, was density, and this is what the developer offered the community: a brand new-apartment that would house a couple hundred new people who would theoretically access the businesses along the main drag, enrol their kids in the community schools, and ride the transit buses out front of their homes.

The neighbours weren't thinking of utilized transit or fuller schools or better local cafés. They were thinking about the mythologized ghettos of New York City and so, inevitably as all fearful people sensibly do, they talked about parking.

"Questions or comments?" the facilitator asked. An active Community League member said, "Your plan has a tiny parking lot in the back for visitors. Hardly enough for that many units."

The developer pointed to the daycare space they had planned at the back of the building. He couldn't confirm a daycare partner to manage this space, but could confirm just how few daycare spots existed in the community.

"Questions or comments?" the facilitator asked. "But what about parking for the staff?" a neighbour who lived across the alley from the daycare asked.

Good God, I thought, the car is killing our collective, creative spirits.

My exasperation doesn't stem from a belief that parking is not a problem to be considered. It's just that so rarely is it the true issue. The neighbourhood had been tricked before; enamoured by other developers' plans that on completion fulfilled half of what they committed to as contractually they aren't obliged to ensure the siding looks like the original model, or that the trees be planted and—if planted—watered, that the daycare not become another couple of units. None of these concerns were essential to the zoning of that property.

Which leads to one of the central problems with developing high density units in older communities: trust. How do communities trust? When we moved into the community, a huge building on 118th Avenue was being built and its design looked promising as there were store front spaces at street level and courtyards with paving stones that hinted at café patios. The first red flag was when the building was cheaply stuccoed with a terrible colour of peach and pastel pink. Then, the property management company appeared to go AWOL as the building was quickly overwhelmed with tenants who cared little for their neighbours and even less for the building. The poorly landscaped courtyards sprouted dandelions and the main floor office users became terrified that bed bugs from above would infest their files and desk chairs.

Parking is one of those bylaws that communities can call on when none of their other concerns—officially—have merit. I don't believe it's wrong for communities to call for good design, or to request that their built environment be both beautiful and utilitarian. In fact, good design and beauty are the principle foundations behind Broken Window Theory, which suggests that the lovelier a space, the more people will rise to care for it.

Two years later, the developer would build a scaled-back version of the model he brought to the meeting in compliance with the neighbours' parking concerns. The building has underground parking and above ground it looks like his initial plan promised: flowers in the front, kids at the back, and people waiting at the bus stop out front.

Miracle upon miracle, there is a wooden fence squared up against the alley and through the slats a play tent and grass where daycare kids kick balls. In a city where some families secure childcare spaces before their children are even born, we lucked out when the developer contracted the YMCA to deck out the bright daycare space with wooden toys, bright costumes, and educational resources. It's close enough to walk and most mornings when we dropped Ali off, we would stroll across the near-empty visitor parking lot and feel grateful we didn't need our car.

11

Smells Like a Deal

WHILE ALBERTA AVENUE has its fair share of great deals on fixer-uppers, it's the second-hand shops where I have found some of my best buys. My strongest memories of shopping as a child are equally split between the bolts of material in Fabricland and rows of clothes in Goodwill. I have tried to pass on the thrift shop memories to my children. Madi had just turned 9, when she began to notice something was different about the second-hand store ten blocks west of our home. We were searching for pants that stretched, that had no tags, that weren't jeans, nor were too tight, nor too long. As I ushered her into the change room with a stack of pants, she said, "Mom, why is all this stuff already used by people?

"Because it's a second-hand store," I said. I fit the dozen pants on one hook leaving another empty for the rejects.

"But why do they sell other people's stuff?" She was still talking, not changing.

"So we can buy it."

"But it smells different in here."

"Then try this stuff on quick so we can leave." This was a point in our relationship—the time when her self-awareness caught up with her powers of intuition—I had been dreading. Granted, she hadn't quite said she would never wear any clothes from here again, but she sounded very close to making that conclusion.

Despite the smell, the city's bed bug problem, and the slim but possible chance of getting scabies or lice, this is one of my favourite places to spend an evening. The Alberta Avenue Value Village is second-rate compared with the Bissell Centre Thrift Shoppe. Six blocks east along 118th Avenue, the pants are always the same price be they Buffalo or Joe. The kids' shoes are usually $1.99 and brand-new books sell for one or two dollars.

The drive for deals is in my blood, passed down through my mother's family to all of the female kin so that when we gather you're bound to hear:

"Love that shirt, Aunt Jo!"

"Yeah? I got it for two ninety-nine at the Goodwill on 51st."

"This chair—is it new?" says a cousin.

"Found it at Sally Anne for five dollars on Discount Saturday." We use the same tone one uses to announce a firstborn child.

To a modest observer, this all may seem a little boastful and garish. I like to think that our spontaneous, unsolicited announcements of both the price and the place of purchase is part of our charm and really, we are just celebrating with each other like communities do.

Take, for instance, the time when I found five Le Creuset cast-iron cooking pots and matching lids tucked slightly back on the Bissell Shoppe's metal shelves. Two of the pots still had stickers on the tan-sometimes-pink-in-certain-lights colour made popular in the 1970s. They had hand-scraped wooded handles with a stainless steel eye hook for easy storage. My organs begin to vibrate as though I had emptied a needle of caffeine directly into my heart. "Stay cool," I coached myself loudly over the noise of my pulse. I had a sudden anxiety that if the staff knew what a deal I had, they would immediately reprice the product, so I forced myself to place the pots in my cart slowly. I even pursed my lips and furrowed my eyebrows at the smallest pot; I rubbed it as though there was some major flaw. No one was watching my theatrics, but I made the motion to put the pot back on the shelf then stopped and tilted my head empathetically, as though to indicate I would adopt the poor thing for its own sake. As I casually took one loop around the store, a quick Internet search confirmed that the whole set retailed for over eight hundred dollars. At the till I paid ten for the lot.

On returning home, I immediately took a photo and texted it to all my friends who cared for me and wanted the best for me. And, I swear I wasn't consciously boasting. My intent was good. There was an element of excited proclamation that can sometimes appear like boasting but really, I was happy and I figured that my friends would be too.

Most of my friends were jealous and another muttered that I "take all the good stuff at the Bissell." I should concede that sometimes thrifting is really cutthroat; like any treasure hunt of significance some poor pirate always gets his hand cut off then his foot cut off but still he manages to swim to shore and kill his best friend who is standing victorious above the trunk of gold.

While it may not bring out the best in people, second-hand shopping can bring the best into my home. No less than a quarter of my belongings are thrifted: my four-piece KitchenAid toaster; most of the frames on my wall; wallets and belts and shoes and dishes and tables. I have bought numerous couches (in fact, at every pregnancy I fancied a different one). However, I stop at buying second-hand beds. I have done it, but I don't like it.

To the uninitiated, this all may seem a little gross. Only occasionally is it that. Like the time I attempted to try on twenty shirts in the dressing rooms with a three-item limit. The rule is there so people don't hog the rooms built with plywood and locked with hook and eye hardware that let light in and the odd flash of breast out. While I didn't respect the limit, I tried to respect the spirit of the rule by hurrying to try on twenty shirts in the space and time another woman would try on three.

Usually I have a system where my clothes hang on the door, the items to try hang on one hook and the items to buy on another. I also have a discard pile that is the thickest and heaviest, but in this change room there weren't enough hooks so I dropped the cotton T-shirt I wore in the corner on the floor. And I am an idiot.

Three shirts and a pair of pants hung on the 'to buy' hook, when Alistair started wailing in the stroller outside my room. He had dropped his toy. My sister, Gini, was a half-inch plywood sheet away from me. "You almost done?" she asked.

"Yeah, just have to put my shirt on." As I pulled the stretch cotton fabric over my head, I gagged and panicked as bile rose in my throat and with my shirt smothered my face until I had the fortitude to push it around my neck.

"Gini?" I swallowed. "I think someone peed in the corner of this change room."

"Ew, I smelled it but didn't know where it could be coming from."

"I didn't notice." Such is the extreme psychological effects of deal hunting that it overwhelms even my sense of smell. "I think I put my shirt in it. And now it's around my neck."

Gini was silent and so was the baby. Gingerly I stretched the neck until it nearly ripped and pulled it over my head as I held my breath. Then I took one of the shirts I meant to buy, put it on and I scrubbed my neck, chin, mouth, and nose with a dozen wet wipes.

At the till I informed the woman who served me regularly that I was wearing a shirt from the store and I felt it should be 'on the house' because mine had soaked up urine.

She shrugged, "Sure."

"You probably should call someone to clean it up," I said.

"Okay."

"It's the last change room on the right."

"Got it."

When I got home I told Mat about it. He stood far back and instead of commiserating he said, "What did you expect?"

I have learned over time and after many purchases to beware of the price on the items locked up at second-hand stores. The glass case at the front of the Bissell Shoppe is filled with a rather jumbled collection that is priced far higher than the goods in the rest of the store: gold-dipped cuff links with fire bolt stampings, water-damaged antique watches, Royal Doulton figurines and costume brooches. Close by is a stand with purses locked to a rack.

One day I popped in to look for wine glasses, which we go through like disposable cups, when I strayed to the rack of bags. A couple other women were fondling a Jimmy Choo white, pleated leather satchel that looked like a smaller version of Mary Poppins' magic carpet bag. My heartbeat sped up slightly as I imagined the original price that was probably as much as the supercalifragilisticexpialidocious carpet bag would get at auction. It didn't occur to me that the bag wasn't real because on a scale where zero is cynical and ten is naive, I am about a seven normally; however, when the adrenaline of deal hunting is released in my brain I come dangerously close to a nine.

The two women were jockeying to touch the bag and I held back. In their late forties, the women wore nylon jackets and socks with sandals, but I knew they could beat the shit out of me if I messed with their deal.

"Angela," they called over the woman who had been flipping through the jackets, the metal hangers scraping the top bar in an even beat broken only as she double-checked the feel of the fabric or the brand tags. She was tall, her black hair hung limply halfway down her back. Her nails were fake with a French manicure and her tiny legs were in jeans covered in cat hair.

"Check out the Jimmy Choo bag, honey," the women called.

"I did. It's a fake." She didn't look up.

"How do you know?" They continued to fondle the bag.

She took the purse from them. Her nails clicked on the metal clasp.

"You need to look on the inside." She pointed to the interior pocket's zipper. "Plastic. An authentic designer bag would never have a plastic zipper."

She moved over to a Coach bag. Now that she had planted the seed of doubt, I remembered the small, square design from a trip to Europe a decade and a half before. There had been dozens of the same purses spread out on blankets or tables in clandestine spaces just off the beaten tourist tracks.

"Deals," the street hawkers would shout. Then I had known the difference between a deal and a scam.

Angela continued inspecting this second specimen. "See the plastic zippers? And look at the embroidered letters of the brand on the outside. They are opaque." She pointed to the bag in the crook of her elbow. "This one's real. It's worth nine hundred new. That is authentic Coach."

"Fake...Fake...Fake...Real," she judged them quickly, pulling open a gaudy black handbag heavy with buckles and hardware. "This one's a good buy. I don't need another one, but it's a great deal." As the women negotiated who would buy the authentic designer bag for $45, I found some crystal wine glasses for fifty cents each and steered clear of the change rooms.

12

Bug Economics

"MY TEACHER TOLD ME that if I tell everyone that I have lice, no one will want to play with me," Madi said as she scratched her head. It sounded like static and made me want to itch too.

"Come here and let me check you again."

"You're like a mama gorilla," she said.

"Yeah, well you're like a baby monkey." At that time she was the only one in the family who had hosted the sneaky insects that feast on small amounts of blood and epidermis. The creatures are sometimes as small as a pin head and look like shrunken crabs in a see-through skin in their early stage of development. As small as they may be, her teacher feared them.

"She screamed at all the girls today," said Madi. This was unusual as Ms. G didn't usually shout at the girls. She saved her higher register for the boys.

"Why?"

"Because we didn't want to put our hair up."

"Like back in a ponytail?"

"Yeah, and I hate having my hair back."

"She just didn't want your hair down, because when your heads and hair touch the lice will spread, right?" Madi knew the bugs couldn't fly or jump very far. She was more concerned about her hair being back than about getting more lice.

Unfortunately, her teacher had a slight phobia around the creatures and her scalp inspections were conducted with two chopsticks that separated the hair to expose the scalp, like Moses parted the seas. Yet if a louse was found, she couldn't simply call the seas back down to drown the prolific creature.

As I methodically parted Madi's hair and looked along the base of her hairline, I realized I had grown to almost like this part of louse hunting. The washing of sheets and pillows and parka hoods and car seat covers I could do without, but the actual act of louse hunting had evolved into a social time and that day, Madi and I sat on the couch for a half hour as I inspected her roots for the nits—lice eggs—set just off the scalp. They look like tiny, grey tears that won't rub off like dandruff might so when I found one, I would tell Madi to breathe and I then pull the hair out along with a few more. If I missed a nit, I knew it would take roughly a week for the tear to pop and for a tiny nymph to emerge. This is the trickiest stage to catch for in this form they are small and virtually invisible except for a small black dot on their backs. They will go through three moults in a week and their small bites and movements will cause the tell-tale scratching. If they can hide from my fingers or metal comb for long enough, they will grow to be the size of a fruit fly and begin to propagate, laying up to eight nits a day for as long as thirty days. If one is not diligent in getting that first tiny louse, the situation can get radically out of control.

"Ms. G found three on Cole today," said Madi. I wondered if he would turn up shaved tomorrow. While lice will move through any and every school, the inner-city schools have a unique challenge. The kill-these-damn-bugs shampoo costs fifteen to twenty dollars per application and often a whole family needs to do it twice to be rid of the bugs. That is, if the shampoo even works. The only other alternative besides the shave of shame is to sit. Carefully. Combing. Pinching. Pulling. Carefully. Combing. Pinching. Pulling.

As I separated the hairs and inspected her pink scalp through glasses that had slid down my nose, I asked, "She was looking at Cole's head while all the other kids were in the class?"

"Yeah, but she only looked for, like, three seconds on my head." She had changed over the past couple of years we had been doing this. While she used to fight, that day she sat with her back straight, her arms still, her voice calm. Relaxed.

||||

My sister-in-law works as an inner city social worker with some of the poorest and most vulnerable folks in the city and while lice are a major problem, bed bugs are even more impossible to control. One summer evening she took a call from a client. "Come, please come over. I can't get to sleep," Jane begged. "I think they are back."

Bobby-Jo promised she would be there in the morning and when she arrived she found her friend pacing the small apartment suite. "I couldn't sleep so I just walked all night. I can't bear the thought of them biting me anymore." The woman's sleep-deprived face creased into sobs that racked her small body. As Bobby rubbed her back, she looked around the room. Along every joint in the rented apartment ran a long line of puffy spray foam. The ceiling was lined with it, the baseboards were double-lined; so were the door-frames and every outlet popping with ugly, yellow insulation. Together they began to search the room, at the duct tape wrapped with the sticky side out, at the syrup in bowls cooling the feet of her furniture, at the tape along the baseboards. There was no sign of fresh bed bugs.

"Jane," Bobby said from the kitchen.

"What, what, you found one?" she jumped out from the other room.

"No, nothing. Just wondering if you want me to make you a cup of tea."

Jane nodded then continued to scour her traps. It had been a month since they had controlled her infestation, a month since she had slept in her bathtub for multiple nights before she could bear the thought of lying on her bed where creatures waited like the bogey man for just the right time to bite.

When the tea was made, Jane announced the traps were all clear, but continued to worry as she nursed her tea.

Bed bugs are resilient creatures that can live for eighteen months without feeding and survive huge variations in temperature between minus sixteen degrees and plus forty-five degrees Celsius. They are insidious and travel anywhere a credit card may go, often along electrical paths and heating systems.

Bed bugs, like lice, aren't a problem limited to the poorer parts of town as they have been found on buses travelling the city and on leather seats in public libraries and in the beds of the ritziest hotels. Theories as to why we have seen a resurgence of these creatures are many and include increased global travel, global warming, over-use and under-use of insecticides. Whatever the reason, my favourite second-hand furniture shop now posts signs informing buyers that twice a week they have a bed bug dog sniff for bugs. It's meant to be reassuring, but it's one of those topics that as soon as you mention it, people begin to scratch.

While everyone can get bed bugs, the poor are most likely to have to deal with the creatures longer than most. If one has money and bed bugs, companies can be hired to heat the house up to temperatures that kills the bugs instantly, saving dozens of trips to the laundry and hardware stores.

If one has a little money and bed bugs, the expensive insecticide, Dr. Doom, works a little more slowly than the instant heat. With a little money, one can pay others to bleach clean the house, or remove a wooden bed, or launder linens and clothes in a hot dryer. Inevitably, some items can't be washed and replacing those items becomes another expense.

Fewer options exist for those who get bed bugs and have no money. It costs money to fight the bugs. It costs money to move. In some instances, people are so desperate, they put themselves in danger by attempting to heat their apartment with propane heaters that explode. Or in the case of one family, two children died of poisoning after their family used insecticide from their home country where ventilation was much greater. While lives aren't often lost, a great deal of mental health and money is.

Bobby-Jo is careful when she goes into the apartments of her clients. She always wears her boots inside and puts her coat in the sink or bathtub. She squats instead of sits. However, when she must sit, she finds a hard-surfaced chair. Yet despite her caution, we got a call from her one weekend morning and she didn't sound well. Bed bugs. She. Found. Bugs. In. Her. Bed.

Mat and I headed over in our nastiest clothes with our stomachs in our mouths. When we arrived Bobby-Jo stopped pacing and waved her arm towards the mattress that leaned against the wall. We knelt down to see the damage to the wooden bed frame. Because her body doesn't react to the bites, the bugs had been able to feed and breed without being noticed until that night she had awoken and spotted a small black bug against her white sheets. When she flipped on the lights, she saw for the first time the tiny dots of blood on the linen and began to hunt for more, which she found in the folds of her mattress and in bug-made trenches in her pine bed frame.

When she called us, she hadn't slept since her discovery and the next few nights she would sleep at our house as the family swarmed the apartment with chemicals and bleach. Black bags went to the garbage and blue bags of linens and clothes went to the industrial driers at the laundromat, which could heat up hot enough and long enough to kill the creatures.

We were extra careful and to kill any errant eggs, we washed with bleach water hundreds of Sharpie pens, picture frames, and wooden bookshelves. Once the bedroom was clear, exterminators came in and sprayed along the baseboards and outlets and doors then instructed her to vacuum every day, multiple times a day, while emptying the container immediately outside in the garbage. There would be a number of battles required to win this war and the first battle required her to lie in her bed as bed bug bait.

Her first night home she drank a bottle of wine and tried to cover her holes. She lay on top of the comforter in thick socks, multiple jogging pants and a hoodie that cinched up tight around her nose. When she closed her eyes she could imagine the bugs going into her vagina, her ears and nose. She imagined them marching like armies across the line of poison. *It will kill them, it will kill them.* She tried to focus on the positive. Eventually, she slept with the images of the small creatures that had begun to spin her life out of control. *I missed one and will have to start this all over again.* Even a year later she would wake up in the middle of the night in panic, turning on the lights to see if she could catch one in the act.

While the anxiety would follow her for a year, so did the stigma of it. She limited where she went for fear she would transfer them. She changed her clothes outside and always worried that if anyone else in her family got bed bugs, we would blame her. She noticed being touched and visited less, and as a natural gift giver, she found herself suddenly self-conscious that every time she gave a gift, people would worry she was transporting bugs.

Five days after we did a full sweep and bleach and spray of her apartment and she hadn't seen any further signs of living bugs, she invited Madi to a celebratory sleepover. Around five in the morning, Madi woke Bobby-Jo up with, "Aunty, look what I found!" Bobby leapt out of bed then reminded herself to freak out on the inside.

"Really, Madi? Let's see," and in the early morning light, she squinted to see a tiny baby bug in Madi's hand. When she looked at Madi's face, she saw the child had a small red bite mark at the end of her nose so for the next three hours until wake-up time they searched for what Madi termed her "friends." They put the dozen or so babies in a Ziploc bag that Aunty promptly disposed of at the child's first distraction.

It would take another few rounds of chemical to rid her suite of the problem. The costs were significant for the inner-city social worker as she needed a new bed, bedding, couch and chairs. Friends bought her the best bed bug mattress cover money could buy and all her new furniture was raised off the floor by legs that could be taped—sticky side out—for early detection. Four years later, because of the nature of her job and because she lives in the same apartment, she remains vigilant. She has become a natural expert, which is probably why she spotted so quickly the bug crawling on one of her client's coats as they discussed his mental health. When the man saw that she saw it, he apologized profusely and stood to leave. "Where are you staying right now?" She asked him gently.

He was sleeping on a couch in a friend's apartment. "They've got a bad problem with the bugs," he told her with his eyes averted, "but it was either stay there or in the shelter, which has them too, or sleep on the street." She knew he probably didn't take his clothes off to sleep.

He left and she called the janitorial staff for help tracking down some Dr. Doom to kill any other errant bugs. She put on a mask and sprayed the office as the custodians who were from different parts of South America watched with some amusement. "What are you scared of? It's just a little bug. Most of the world has bugs like this." They told her to tape the legs of her chairs and bed, then went into detail about the various household remedies used back home to keep control of the insects. For them, the problem was one to manage, not eradicate.

Her client didn't visit her office for two weeks from embarrassment and when he came back, he spoke to her from outside her door. Remembering her own stigma, she said, "Come in. Talk to me. Did you find a new place?"

13

Food Politics

Hi Neighbour,

We would like to share some important news of a proposed development in our area. The Salvation Army has been approved to build a new building on their current location.

The Salvation Army was denied a request last year to build a "religious assembly" building because the Development Officer deemed it to be used for "Community Recreation Services," because of the social services expected to be offered, including a soup kitchen. This decision was upheld at the Subdivision and Development Appeal Board in October. However, they reapplied and have now received approval (from a different Development Officer) to construct a "religious assembly" which we believe is still intended for the purposes of predominantly social services.

We are concerned with the negative impacts this development is likely to have on our community. We stopped by with a petition in support of our appeal opposing the re-development of the Salvation Army on 95th Street. We're sorry we missed you.

If you would like to sign the petition or would like more information, please send us an email with your name and address and a time that would

*work for you. Let us know if you would like to be kept up to date on the
progress or would like to be more involved.*

Thanks so much for your time.

The letter was unsigned.

Many of the homeless in Alberta Avenue migrated to get away from
downtown where they felt more vulnerable to abuse and violence. For
years their destination was the Salvation Army church just a block north
of the library and a block south of Alberta Avenue. The church had served
regular, free meals and hosted Narcotics and Alcoholics Anonymous
meetings for decades when they opened a winter warming centre funded
by the City. On nights when temperatures fell below minus twenty
degrees Celsius, they would open the building all night. There were no
cots, but often people fell asleep on the hard chairs with their arms
pillowed under their heads.

The Salvation Army's pink stucco building had aged badly. Eventually
city inspectors ordered them to stop serving food from their kitchen,
then they were then informed that the building was a health hazard and
so they decided to demolish and rebuild. The people and programs of
the church moved two blocks south along 95th Street into Bethel Bible
Chapel, which agreed to share its building.

The Salvation Army hired a premier design firm to draw up the
blueprints for a new building that would be no bigger than the original,
but far more accessible. When it came time to obtain building permits,
however, they came face to face with angry neighbours who worried the
Salvation Army was a draw for criminal elements in the city. Someone
had reported seeing a sex act on the property, and others had reported
drug dealers and garbage from take-out dinners. The church's first
request was denied, so when it came time to go forward for a second time,
they tried to garner support from the community.

I was at the meeting of the Community League's board when the
captain (that is what they call their pastors) arrived with her architect.

In his arms was a model of the modern-looking building that would stretch across the lot, let ample sunlight into the main area and provide an accessible kitchen for those in wheelchairs. The seven or eight board members sat around two eight-foot tables pushed together.

The Salvation Army's presentation was first on the agenda, and they requested a letter of support from the league, which they hoped would move development permits along more smoothly. The captain explained that the church didn't want to add square footage, but wanted to reduce the number of stairs and build a more suitable kitchen for community dinners where everyone would be welcome. The architect pointed out the LED lighting at the back and sides to discourage loitering and heavy bushes along the perimeter to discourage sleeping.

The members of the board weren't convinced by the captain's talk of church community nor the building's improved design. Their main concern, mirrored by the anonymous campaign letter in my mailbox, was that the Salvation Army functioned like a service agency and not a church and, the neighbours continued, this service agency was a very bad neighbour.

||||||

A decade before, I worked for a similarly described bad neighbour. The Mustard Seed Street Church was a service organization just ten blocks south housed in an old church whose steeple was exclusively used by pigeons and whose exterior bricks were slowly disintegrating into fine powder. The main steps were deeply grooved from a century of visitors, first German Baptist congregation members whose numbers had surged then dwindled, then late-night partiers hoping for a good time at a local country star's bar, and now the poorest in the city.

When I started as a summer student in the early two thousands there were ten staff who met every morning, united by our willingness to work for little pay if the cause was just. I was still paid twice the average annual earnings of most guests who arrived for meals, lounged in the plastic chairs to suffer through another round of karaoke just to stay out of the cold or delay returning to their bed bug-ridden bed or watch the washrooms for their dealer to drop an eight ball that would soothe whatever emotional torment needed it.

We were like the Salvation Army in that we didn't like to call those who joined the block-long meal lines or those who accessed our clothes pantry or coffee bar clients. We hoped that they would be more than that: that they would come for lunch and stay for a board game, or book club, or karaoke, or Sunday church. In the early days AA meetings met throughout the week and the building was open all night long to support the women and men working the corners. Almost all of the staff were volunteers from the inner city.

In the early days, the organization was a church where the city's most vulnerable people gathered jointly to meet their spiritual and social needs, but it wasn't long before the physical and emotional needs of visitors expanded beyond what a small group of people could handle. Lunch lines swelled to two hundred people and Friday dinners to five hundred. Requests for mittens, sleeping bags, items for the kids' lunches grew and people needed socks, deodorant, toothbrushes, and socks, socks, socks.

The church began to search for donors. Leftover bits of cooked ham from a convention dinner would show up, along with beans and perhaps some gardener's bumper crop of potatoes and it all went in the soup pot. Of course, food drew more people and more people meant more needs. The Mustard Seed asked its supporters for household items: for blankets and backpacks and socks and mittens. People responded with truck-loads of stuff that filled the upper balconies and every other empty space the church had. When staff went on vacation, their office would fill up too. The donations were a relief because now one didn't have to turn people away knowing that tomorrow morning the frostbite would have claimed fingers. The donations also complicated the work and relationships. Staff and volunteers had come to connect to people but they soon became marshals of stuff: cold-hearted misers defensive that they were being used and whose quiet inner voices began not to ask, "What can I do for you?" but "What do you want from me?" and "How are you lying to me?" Trust broke down over a pair of Dollarama socks.

In only a few years the organization moved from a church of like-minded parishioners working to mutually enhance one another's lives, to a service agency where the hierarchy of power that existed in the prisons, in social services, and in the schools was generally replicated.

I stayed on after my summer student gig ended and sported six job titles over the next six years. In year two, I was tasked with expanding the dinner program from two to six nights a week, and ending our lunch program. Lunches had been served Sundays through Fridays for a decade and were exactly what one imagined a soup line to look like. Folks stood outside the metal doors and the line-up stretched down the front ten steps, through the building's parking lot and around into the back alley.

Almost all of the time, the line was a friendly place to be. Many of the soup line attendees had a long history together and with the Seed, like one couple who had been partners for two decades and contributed count-less hours a week serving coffee, preparing snacks, and cleaning tables.

Another woman, in her sixties with red hair, who lived five doors north, wore jeans studded with diamonds and sported manicured nails that clicked as she cleaned the sugar jars and transferred the mugs to the kitchen. Sometimes she would take extra food and clothes to her basement suite and it never occurred to her that it was stealing until she was informed that any more of it would revoke her volunteer status. Staff told her, "If you need it, just ask, okay?" She volunteered at our Sunday church services, cheerfully working the projector during the singing though she never seemed to know when to switch pages or pull the lyrics back down to the top when we hit the chorus again. It was at least six months I worked with her in the food bank before I realized she struggled to read.

In line, there was also one of the shyest men I've met who came only to our lunch meals because it was during daylight hours and meant there were fewer people than at our evening meals. Every time I saw him he would say, "Oh, oh, oh look at you and that pony tail of yours."

And he would reach up tentatively to pat my head. "You got a bit of a bald spot there, Carissa. Yes, Yes." It didn't matter if I had long or short hair, a ponytail or not, he would pat my head with his hands covered in thin, cotton gloves winter or summer. He always left with soap, which he hoarded to later use in the fight against the day's marauding germs.

There was Cowboy Carl who wore a hat with pins that said, "Lose weight now, Ask me how!" For the first four years we lived in Alberta Avenue, I would see Carl swinging his briefcase and striding confidently along. He moved with an air of irreverence at the construction that transformed his regular routes into brick-layered, green-treed trails.

I knew him as "Uncle Carl." He was the relative of one of our volunteers and an infectious optimist. On Monday most nouns were prefaced with "Marvellous!" There were Super Sundays and Fabulous Fridays. When he was a child, frequent violent seizures left him sometimes unconscious and always disoriented. He finished grade 3 then reported that the school refused to teach him so he learned to read and write at home. After moving to the city, he lived in various forms of poorly managed housing: mostly rooming houses and basement suites. He ate at the "safer" downtown charities, but no matter where he lived or dined, his briefcase, shiny as a freshly buffed army boot, accompanied him. Inside was a place mat and disposable cup saved from his morning coffee at the mall food court. "There's no point in tossing a perfectly good cup," he would always say. A seizure killed him one night in his suite in a poorly managed building along 118th Avenue.

There was Sound-Guy Warren, and Jean-Jacket Larry. There was the silent Bird Man who didn't speak, but could communicate very clearly. Once I refused to give him a hammer and he wrote with his finger on the icy door, "FU HO." He spoke only once in our hearing to a staffer dressed up for Halloween in a costume he perhaps mistook for an angel. She was shaking him awake when he sat up and started talking with an Eastern European accent. He had come to Canada as a body builder, he had been a vegetarian for years, he had a son, and he often walked to the outskirts of the city to sleep because it was safer. It was the first and last time any of us heard him speak.

These constants from the community were the true hosts. As new staff filed in for experience and filed back out for experience elsewhere, this core group of regulars reminded people of the rules, informed the culture, and made a disorienting place feel like a safe space for countless nervous volunteers and naive staff.

In our shift out of lunches and into dinners we considered our need for more volunteers and kitchen capacity. We considered staff, building access, and the folks needing our meal lines. However, how the surrounding neighbourhoods and communities would be affected remained a distant consideration. The organization worked hard to get through the days without a critical incident and through the month with enough money in the bank to pay the staff; at the time no one had time to consult.

It soon became clear that the lunch lines had gone largely unnoticed by the majority of the residents of the McCauley neighbourhood, a community directly south of Alberta Avenue, people with day jobs. The dinner lines, however, made the poverty, vulnerability, and occasional violence much more visible. Not only were there more people in line, but neighbours now were home to see the lines and everything else that came with it. The Seed's styrofoam takeout containers hung like leaves in the winter-nude caragana hedges. Napkins waved like small white surrender flags from the boulevard bushes. People would meet at the Seed and, in groups, move loudly and hysterically with no destination through the alleys and streets off 96th Street. Fights broke out, as they sometimes do when a lot of people gather then disperse and the Mustard Seed had limited plans or resources for crowd control beyond its property.

Many in McCauley felt resentment and anger similar to the Alberta Avenue Community League board's feelings about the Salvation Army's programs. However, while the Mustard Seed continues to operate, Sally Ann's boarded up building sinks slowly into the corner lot that grows wilder with every passing month.

Sometimes when the children are at school and the house is too quiet or dirty to work in, I take my laptop and sit at one of the dining-sized tables at Sprucewood library a block from home. It's a busy place with Wi-Fi and a bank of computers people can use for free. Natural light floods the children's section complete with touch screens, books, games, and an electric train that circles on a track hanging from the ceiling. The usual collection of books, CDs, and magazines flank the north and east walls while the bank of computers set in the centre of the library are always full. On the south of the building, a community meeting room hosts weekly programming where Lily learned to sing *Twinkle, Twinkle* and Ali saw his first puppet show. This library is one of the few places outside of downtown where people without homes can go when temperatures dip like high divers into a pool now that the Sally Anne's winter warming shelter is closed.

One November afternoon I sat down at the table with three women who had stripped from their wet winter gear and sat reading old copies of British gossip rags. A middle-aged man entered the library and quickly made his way to our table.

"Dale gave all his blankets away," he said with some urgency to the matriarch sitting across from me. He literally steamed from the temperature change. "Did you hear me?" the man asked his friend. "Dale gave away all his blankets so I have to walk back downtown to get him some more."

He stood with a slight stoop and focused on the woman who occasionally acknowledged him with a nod into the pages of her *Hello! Canada*. Princess Kate was having another baby and her morning sickness was awful. "Oh no," she said at the same time as she turned the page. Her slender brown fingers, short nails and slightly swollen knuckles turned the next page to reveal a spread of another European royal family.

Next to her a younger, heavier woman read *Majesty*. She didn't respond to Dale's plight at all because just then a wracking cough took her breath away and forced a spray of spit across the article. I wondered if she had tuberculosis and whether I would be wise to move.

"Don't you go out until later, okay?" He had a hand now on the *Hello!* pages and the elder finally gave him her full attention. "The library's open until nine. So stay here until then, okay?"

"Yes." Her voice was low and slightly muffled by the high collar on her sweater. She rubbed her hands. "Your arthritis," he said, patting her hands. "This cold must be hurting you. I'll try to be back before nine, but I've got to go downtown. Dale gave away all his blankets."

"Now why'd he do that?" she asked as though her tongue had thawed.

"He said the other guy needed them more." He kissed her. "Stay warm."

I left before he got back, passing a couple of cars in which drivers sat accessing the free Wi-Fi. The wind was sharp on my nose and teased tears out only to freeze them. I had reached our alley when it occurred to me that the next day was a statutory holiday. The library would be closed, and the group would need to find some other shelter besides the library and besides the Sally Ann. They would probably all be walking down to the Mustard Seed.

14

Local Sex Economics

THE KIDS' BUS STOP was three blocks away from home and I usually enjoyed the end-of-the-work-day ritual of walking to pick them up. One October day, I made an effort to march so that the leaves under my feet crunched like potato chips. I was the first parent to reach the bus stop and I waited a few minutes in the leaves before another mother showed up. She was younger than me by almost a decade and wore cotton pants with a Hello Kitty print and an oversized hoodie that hid her body and hair.

We greeted each other with our eyes, smiled, then turned our attention to the leaves. We waited a few more minutes and a cop passed. The car crept by and then stopped in the intersection. He rolled down his window and called, "You ladies waiting for anything?"

I stared at him a little confused until it dawned on me that perhaps I should be happy he was cruising the side streets. I thought briefly that I should find it all very funny, but instead of laughing I said slowly: "We're waiting for our children to come off the bus. Like from school."

He was just doing his job.

For those of us not involved in buying or selling sex, we regularly see the desperation of the sellers and the casualness of the buyers. We walk past the condoms, and sometimes we must speed up so as not to be hassled by johns.

My parents live a few blocks north off the main sex stroll of 118th Avenue in a bi-level bungalow on a street lined by fifty-year-old trees and five-year-old trucks. My dad was reading in the backyard one afternoon when shrieking and banging from his alley interrupted the novel's plot line. He went to investigate and found a woman across from his back gate howling with anger that bounced off his garage door into his serene yard of roses and sweet peas. The tiny woman in tights and a T-shirt began to slam herself into his neighbour's metal garage door.

"Excuse me." He cleared his throat.

No reaction.

"Excuse me," he said a little louder. "Can I help you?"

He moved into the back alley so she could see him, and she promptly walked off. As Dad looked around for a cause, Neighbour Guy, whose garage she was bouncing off, sauntered over. He is half Dad's age and often stops to talk about stuff that shouldn't happen outside of a Cineplex Odeon screen. This time was no different except that Neighbour Guy had a confession to make: it was his fault that she was so mad, he said but he couldn't help it because he just couldn't pay her.

"Couldn't pay her for what?" I asked my dad later that evening.

"For sex. He said he wouldn't pay her because she wouldn't do it how he liked."

"What did he want?"

Dad shrugged. It was Mom that later filled me in on the intimates. "She wouldn't let him bite her nipples."

I could see why Dad struggled to say that out loud to his eldest daughter. I too could understand the woman's anger.

||||||

The street sex trade along Alberta Avenue and some of its subsidiaries is a very active one, and loss of payment is one of the less brutal risks the women take selling sex on the street. Between 1993 and 2015, thirty sex workers went missing from the streets of central Edmonton neighbourhoods and were found murdered. Despite the dangers, often the most desperate women continue to hit these streets where the money is low compared to what can be made as an escort or in the clubs and massage parlours.

For a while, signs were posted on lamp standards along 95th Street and 118th Avenue: "This community does not tolerate prostitution," they read, followed by the Report-A-John number. Without any irony, many of the women went on working the same corners now festooned with these metal wagging fingers. I imagine the signs scared off the odd sex buyer, but like the plastic owl set on a roof to scare off pigeons, without immediate consequences the johns came back.

The creeping johns often motivated the crime-prevention group who met every Tuesday at the Carrot Coffeehouse to discuss grassroots crime-prevention strategies. One spring morning the group sat around one of the longer tables close to the door, propped open for the first time all year, allowing the odd note or right-handed melody to drift in off the keys of the purple, public piano sitting on the corner. I sat in one of the donated, over-stuffed leather chairs and listened to them earnestly discuss bylaw infringements related to a discarded mattress on a lawn.

While I should have been typing, I found myself distracted by a woman outside the window. She was eye-catching: full-bodied with undergarments that brought out her curves and voluminous, dark hair that nearly reached her mini, shiny silver shorts. From her wide hips extended black mesh legs capped with ankle-high grey leather boots.

"Check out our neighbourhood greeter," said one regular, looking over his bifocals with a tight, derisive smile.

"Now *those* are some short shorts," said a senior. One of the women gave him a disapproving glance.

As we watched, she was rejected by a guy in a ball cap driving a white Ford. An older beater truck rounded the corner for the second time and this time the driver stopped and she crossed the street oblivious to the table of people with their pens out ready to take the guy's license plate number.

From my view, it's always a bit tricky to report a john. One has to have a pen or a good memory and in this day of camera phones and Google, who has that? One can snap pictures of license plates, but I am always nervous about getting caught. The guy has a vehicle and most likely a lot to lose so do I really want to look so obvious about narking him—and her—out? These community activists didn't appear concerned; there was safety in numbers and the plate glass window of the café. As the truck peeled away, the group couldn't agree on whether the man was young or old. Then a cry rose from the table. In the john's rush to escape the café's scanning eyes, he had run right into a stabilization cable rooting one of the utility poles in the alley to the ground hooking his old, loose bumper to the cable. He rushed to free himself while she casually sat in the cab and I hoped for her sake that her meter was ticking.

The table emptied into the street making the john fumble even more and as the group chortled openly about his "skills," the middle-aged guy in loose-fitting jeans kicked the bumper hard and finally bent it free. He ran as best as his heavy set body could around the front of his truck and as he drove away, he spun his tires in lame protest. As the group filed back into the Carrot they bemoaned the state of the community, city, province, world, but it's not like any of this is new. I have heard it said that prostitution is the oldest profession in the world, yet I met a former sex worker who dryly observed: "I'm pretty sure that the oldest profession is farming."

Over a century ago, sex for money was also an issue in this community. According to *The Edmonton Bulletin*, a "vigilance committee" in Norwood presented evidence in court that the police were allowing a fully operational bordello to continue while the police chief insisted the houses had been shut down. The truth was, *The Bulletin* said, that once or twice a year the keepers and "inmates" of the houses were hauled before an inspector where they would plead guilty and be fined ten to fifteen dollars for keepers, and five to ten dollars for inmates. Then everyone would be on their way because, really, how can one stop a trade agreement that has been going on as long as anyone can remember?

Kate Quinn, whom I've met on a number of community and work-related projects, has spent the last three decades considering this question and as we walked along 118th Avenue she told me her story. She and her family endured years of men parking alongside their house to turn tricks with girls and women before a sex worker frantically pounded on her door one night in the deep winter just as she and her husband were headed to bed upstairs where their two young boys slept soundly. Their home was tucked at the end of a no-thru road where the road became a path that wound behind the football stadium. On nights when no game is on, the stadium is a giant rising from a black hole of empty parking lot and the dark and privacy made the side curb of Kate's house a favourite for men wanting to have sex in their cars. The condoms were thrown out the driver's side of the car for Kate and her husband to clean up.

That night she opened the door to a woman standing on their doorstep in the cold, and behind her Kate took in the silhouettes of two men at the end of the walk. Kate instinctively pulled her into the house.

"What's happening?" Kate asked

"Those guys, I'm afraid," the young woman said.

"Should we call the police?"

"No," the woman said. "I don't think they'll help me."

"Okay," Kate said. "Then how about a cup of tea?"

As they waited for the men to dissolve into the Stadium property, the shaking teacup warmed the woman's hands. The woman's home was just a few blocks away from Kate's.

Kate asked her if her husband could drive her home and as the women finished her tea, he went out to heat the car. The headlights turned on and illuminated the men crouched behind their garage, waiting for their neighbour.

"I can't imagine what they would have done with her," said Kate. Thirty years had passed and she still could visualize the woman's fear that would mark a turning point for Kate as a woman. *What is the same between me and her? What is different? What can women with different life experiences do to bring about change? Are there ways to work together?* The search for answers would drive her for the next three decades.

While the late-night tea was her first face-to-face with a woman selling sex in her neighbourhood, she would meet many more over the next few years of activism. In 1992 she quit her job as an educator with an international development agency. Kate felt her elementary school boys needed her around more and so, as she looked around at what else she could do, she noticed the rapid rise in the visible street sex trade on the corners and in the alleys of McCauley. The sex strolls had generally been downtown, but a revival of night life and new development in the downtown began to push the sex sellers north and east. Some sex trade activity was located around one of the larger truck dealers in the city. The dealer didn't like the idea that their trucks might be associated with that kind of "pick up" so they pressed the police, who pressed the women eastward.

At the height of it in the late eighties and early nineties, Kate could be in her front yard in the mid-afternoon and to her right was sex in a car, while to her left her boys played tag. The children were oblivious but for how long? The neighbourhood began to organize and reached out to other inner city community leagues to work together with the question: How could they not just move it, but stop it?

Community meetings around the issue started as early as 1989. They strategized about how to reduce the problem but they also talked about what the problem really was. They invited outreach and safe house workers to educate them, along with police officers, student lawyers, parents whose daughters were being exploited on Edmonton streets, and finally, women with past experience in the sex trade. They held discussions that helped them answer the question: What activity causes the most harm to the most people? The answer was the activity of the "johns," the sex buyers. It was their cruising and lurking and harassing that put girls and women at risk, impacted community life and exploited vulnerable girls and women, so they began targeting sex buyers with regular "Action Against John" walks. Anyone who volunteered with their group signed on to be nonviolent, nonjudgemental, nonconfrontational, whether with the buyers and sellers of sex or the pimps and traffickers (sex traders). They were there for the safety of their community, not to be vigilantes.

The activists' focus would turn to McCauley School, which sat in the middle of the community. The brick school building, now a vibrant multi-cultural centre, along with the playground and soccer field, take up an entire city block, across from family homes and bordered by alleys on the east and west, 107th Avenue to the north. This main thoroughfare brings traffic in and out of downtown to the eastern communities. No one really knows who came first, the women selling or the men buying, but by 1989 the traffic around the school was disproportionately *not* school traffic. Turning off the main drag, cars would bump into the alleys then slowly troll the block's circuit.

The school housed both elementary and junior high kids and all ages found themselves targeted by inquiring johns. Girls and boys. Were they selling? Mothers dropping children off. Were they selling?

The community action group began to search out the scale of the problem and to ensure it wasn't just in their heads, they counted. The city figured that on a normal day, given the residences and the school, there should be six to seven hundred cars a day moving along the street at the front of the school. Their count tallied three thousand seven hundred cars in one twenty-four-hour period. In many of the vehicles sat lone men, buying whatever there was to sell in front of an elementary/junior high school.

Matters reached a boiling point at a police commission meeting where the commission faced three hundred angry people who bluntly asked the police for help (not much different than in 1908 when the Norwood community begged the same). Residents hadn't gotten much response before and many in the community assumed it was because the police liked that the block contained the sex trade. The theory was that it was an easier beast for the police to manage when the trade was isolated to one, tidy area.

The week after the raucous commission meeting, the police chief announced that 1992 would be the Year of the John. The police service committed to arrest five hundred johns that year. The activism also led to cement barricades on 96th Street and double one-way signs that prevented traffic from circulating around residential streets, avenues and alleys. It led to police crackdowns and fines and soon the trade moved, slowly at first, then more quickly it spread out onto the streets north, east and beyond down the artery of 118th Avenue.

Kate and her neighbours watched their victory with a heavy feeling in their chests. While she had campaigned at the school and monitored the trade, she had interacted with the women. She had even gotten to know some johns and it upset her that most of the men seemed to have no idea of how their method of purchase might affect the women from whom they bought sex, nor the community in which they bought it.

Further, the police service had done additional work assessing the scope of the problem and they identified over two hundred and fifty children and teens and seven hundred and fifty adults selling sex on street corners in the inner city neighbourhoods.

Those numbers and the people she met led Kate further into research on what drove the girls, women, and men into the trade. She went to meetings and seminars. A small social justice group began to grow beyond just interested neighbours to include women who had left the sex trade and parents of women in the sex trade. Her questions expanded: what is it like to be a fourteen-year-old boy with an older sister selling sex? What is it like to be a dad whose daughter is being abused by other men? What can you do as a parent to protect your kids from selling *and* buying?

"All of us are affected," she told me as we walked along 118th Avenue. We passed one strung-out woman and Kate said, "If your family is on the street, if you are buying sex, if you are selling sex, as community and taxpayers we all pay one way or the other."

Beyond their grassroots community meetings, city council created an action group on prostitution that was chaired by the mayor, and active committees branched off this group looking at social factors that led to the sex trade and how this changed neighbourhoods.

In 1995, The John School in San Francisco came to the attention of one of the Alberta Avenue members of the community group, who had watched a feature on the Oprah show. Two police officers were sent to observe the school, and when they came back, a meeting was organized at Alberta Avenue Community Hall to learn about their findings alongside former sex workers, community activists, and parents of women on the street agreed that the john school would be an effective program for Edmonton to help decrease the harmful impact on all concerned. This was then brought to decision-makers—the police chief, the assistant deputy minister of justice, and the mayor.

The officers presented the premise of the school set up as an alternative measures program for johns arrested for the first time. They had to complete a one-day workshop about the sex trade's harm. Fines from the johns were rerouted to pay for the school, which scheduled talks by former sex workers, former sex buyers, and families of sellers and buyers, along with crown prosecutors, police, public health educators, neighbourhood residents and small business owners.

The Edmonton officials agreed to develop the systems to make it happen. Fees that were the equivalent of fines were implemented and rerouted to the community who formed a nonprofit group to administer the money and the school. Kate, who had experience in advocacy and adult education, became the leader of the program and she has led it through two decades. The organization has expanded beyond educating johns to reaching out to sellers, to supporting affected families, and advocating for national laws that would make the exploitation of vulnerable persons illegal.

The offices of Kate's organization, now called Centre to End All Sexual Exploitation (CEASE), is a nondescript building on 118th Avenue. There is no sign on the front and the light-mint stucco is grey from the grit of the Avenue. The front bay windows peek into small offices with metal chairs and laminated tables on steel legs. It's not a drop-in for women seeking safe haven, but rather a hub for organizing and I met her there just three blocks from my house.

From the crusty windows Kate watches the Avenue. Last summer she saw a man stop and pick up a woman who had been working the streets for over ten years. She was barefoot in ripped jeans with an active mental health issue. "Can't you see that this woman is vulnerable?" she shouted at him from her second floor office. To me she said, "The men can pick out who is vulnerable—and *that* should be the crime."

Her vision is for a Canada where "we won't tolerate the exploitation of vulnerable persons at any age or any gender for purposes of sexual exploitation," Kate said. "The old understanding of 'prostitution' assumes the status quo—the selling of sex—and created laws from that starting point, historically focusing the legal weight and public opinion negatively on the sellers of sex services. Rarely were questions asked about why a person might be selling sex. People cast moral judgements rather than confronting the tough social, economic, and patriarchal issues. What about the role and impact of the other parties—the sex buyers and pimps, traffickers, profiteers?"

On my short walk home I passed a couple of the "This neighbourhood does not tolerate prostitution" signs. When they were initially installed on 118th Avenue, Kate petitioned for different wording and on walks along 95th Street you can see her influence. The signs there read "This neighbourhood does not tolerate exploitation."

From her vantage point, the word "exploitation" doesn't focus the negative attention on the women like "prostitution" does. We had stood in the CEASE offices where she reasoned, "Many people still think of the prostitute first when they see the term 'prostitution' and not the buyer or the pimps and traffickers. Nor does the word prostitute force us to consider how we are all complicit in the exploitation of persons in vulnerable circumstances." She paused and looked to the east, down the avenue from where so many women had disappeared and ultimately lost their lives. "I profoundly believe that our collective conversations must begin at a different starting point, one with social justice at its heart."

15

Rub and Tug
in the City

WHEN PEOPLE ASK ME if the sex trade on the corner of my street bothers me, I say that it does. But it's not because I am particularly worried for my kids' safety or that I believe the sale of sex should be prohibited. What bothers me is the vulnerability of many sellers and the abuse of power by many pimps and buyers. I once watched a teen jump out of a truck wearing a hoodie, panties, and high black boots. As she ran against a red light at the intersection where I was stopped she tried to pull her hoodie over her bottom. Her legs were black with bruises that could have been one bruise except for the bursts of yellow hinting at different contact points. I saw her the next day and she had pants on, but wore the same hoodie pulled over her hair that couldn't hide her face mottled black and blue like her legs.

Those bruises bother me. Her coked out eyes bother me. And her buyers who left their homes from all over the city to pick up an under-age girl in trucks and minivans—some with seats still warm from the bodies of their children recently dropped off at school—they bother me too.

But not all women start out or even end up selling sex on the streets as much of the trade happens indoors, generally unregulated. Kendra had sought help from Kate Quinn's organization. She spoke to a group of women I met with irregularly to have a drink and discuss pertinent issues of the day. She looked like many of us, had a kid like many of us, was working on a degree, like many of us.

Kendra's entrance into the sex trade was through an ad on the back pages of the newspaper that promised two thousand dollars a week at a time when she desperately needed it. Her condo had flooded and was stripped to the studs, but she had no money to finish the reconstruction. The last year she had worked five part-time jobs: as a personal trainer, a waitress, a car detailer and unfortunately, none of the jobs had paid the Canadian Revenue Agency enough tax so she faced a ten thousand dollar debt to the Tax Man. Then, there was the misfortune of her ex-boyfriend's final fuck you: he had disappeared with his coke habit and another ten thousand from her line of credit.

At the moment she read the ad, she found herself without any job because, the week before, she had quit them all to take a position with Correctional Services of Canada. Unfortunately, the day before she was to start, an earlier, nastier ex had phoned her cell.

Corrections Canada called her soon after.

"Did a man named X call you?"

"Yes, he's an ex-boyfriend. He was abusive and I've been trying to shake him for years. I don't know how he got my new number."

He had called her from a federal penitentiary, the official said. Guards couldn't have relationships with inmates so her job offer was off the table.

||||||

She was sleeping alone in a condo without drywall, and a stack of bills sat next to the fridge that contained a box of baking soda and some vinegar. Looking into that fridge, at the emptiness, her future yawned as one big, black hole. She needed to do something before gravity disappeared so she picked up the phone and dialled the number in the ad. A woman answered her inquiry about a job. "I can't talk on the phone. You have to come in."

The address was on an industrial strip of 118th Avenue. Inside, mouse droppings and cigarette stains greeted her. The proprietor was cagey. "You want a job?"

"Well, you haven't really told me about what it is you do."

"You don't know what we do here?" There was a long hallway with a number of small rooms, each with a raised bed covered in cracked vinyl where stuffing came out and God-only-knows-what went in. The sign outside flashed something about a Club.

"Hand jobs, right?" she said with a nervous laugh. She was twenty-one and she had heard about massage parlours; "rub and tugs" they were called.

The proprietor stared hard at her. "We fuck for money here."

It took her breath away. "But aren't there jobs that don't require *that*? Reception, maybe?"

"We fuck for money here." The proprietor was direct to a fault.

"I have to think about it," she said. *I'm not coming back here.*

"See you in a week," the proprietor said.

In a week she was back with the stage name Kendra. She trembled with apprehension; she had never done anything like this before. Well, she had had sex, but never for money and never with a stranger. Her first time was when she was fourteen with a guy in his twenties. His pestering for sex had been annoying, so she figured she would get the whole virginity thing over with. After that there had been a few steady boyfriends and each lasted a couple of years through her teens. When she moved to Edmonton, she was running from a guy who had abused drugs and her body; it was this same guy whose phone call would later make her lose the one job that offered to pay above ten dollars an hour.

The first day she asked the proprietor about what she was supposed to do in the room, and the woman, who hadn't been particularly helpful up to this point despite her clairvoyance that Kendra would be back, told her to get a proper Body Rub Practitioner business license from the city which would cost her two hundred and fifty dollars. When she asked again about her job responsibilities, the proprietor waved her arms. "I can't tell you that. I could be criminally charged."

"But I thought you said it's legal?"

"Well, it is, but I can't give you instructions." She wasn't Kendra's boss; she was simply renting Kendra a room for forty bucks a customer and Kendra was an independent operator who should have her own policies, procedures, and pricing.

There were other women working at the parlour and Kendra asked them what the hell she was supposed to do with a strange man for one hour in a small room with a locked door. The questions chased apprehension up her spine and wound tight around her lungs. The women didn't want to share their tips: she was competition.

Neither was her background particularly helpful in preparing her for the week that lay ahead. She grew up in a rich oil town in the North; her parents had both earned six-figure salaries. She had never been sexually abused. She had never had a drug habit (despite the proclivities of the men she dated). Her first client argued with her about her fee.

"Two hundred and twenty dollars for an hour," she said.

"You can't get that. You're new here."

She held her ground. "Two hundred and twenty."

Her first client was rough and despite their negotiation, he shoved one hundred and eighty dollars into her hand before stalking off.

Stepping out for a cigarette, she was shaking. Did that really happen? She couldn't believe she had just made money having sex. It had felt wrong. But she had enough money from one hour of work to pay her phone bill that month and it would have taken her over fifteen hours of personal training to make what she had just made in an hour. She felt giddy. Dirty and giddy: feelings that had never really gone together for her before.

That night she would have intercourse with four different men and that night would turn into a year at that parlour. When she moved, it was to another parlour, which had modern decor and clean rooms, but the men were far more rough. Three years later, Kendra moved again, this time downtown where the clients were wealthy and mostly kind. By then, her debts were paid off and yet she couldn't seem to stop. Now she was thinking about buying a car and she had other ambitions that required money: school, a house, a family.

Four years after that first night, she decided to get her own shop. She found a great deal on office space and recruited some friends from other shops who rented rooms from her and worked alongside her. Seven years after her first night, she had finished a degree and found a man who wanted to spend his life with her. Finally she sold the store. After seven years in an industry she entered knowing nothing about, Kendra had had sex for money with 4,300 men.

She made (and largely spent) $1.2 million.

She had travelled to the beach, bought a car and paid for school.

She had been choked and raped. She had been stalked and followed. She had been asked to defecate into mouths, pee into cups, role play a man's nine-year-old sister whom he used to molest (one of the very few times she called the police).

Kendra isn't called Kendra anymore. She again uses her birth name and has added a married name. She is tanned and funny, fit and intelligent and now speaks to johns, and groups like ours not forced by court order to listen and who are prepared to be rallied.

"I believe this industry should be abolished and that indoors isn't much safer than outdoors," she said to the women sitting rapt in a west-end coffee shop, pointing out ID of clients was never taken. "Also, I believe the city needs to register women, instead of license them. Our city needs an advocate to work with the women interested in getting into the business: someone who can help navigate some of the initial challenges that bring the women to that place."

||||

Kendra's story is set in a mostly "legitimate" sex trade, but many women still sell sex without the permission of the city's licensing department. Over the last ten years of living here, I have seen an ebb and flow of women waiting for tricks on street corners in Alberta Avenue. The sex trade has visibly reduced on 118th Avenue and Kate suggests it's not because of the signs that read "This community does not tolerate prostitution." Nor is it due to the occasional sit in where residents take over the street corners with Monopoly games and cello concerts. In this age of the Internet, just as you can order toilet paper from Amazon and fine wines direct from the vineyard, so too can you order sex, delivered to your door, any time of the day and night. Johns don't need to visibly cruise the neighbourhood anymore if they have access to a phone with 3G.

The Internet ads make the old classifieds in the Calgary Sun that I studied as a ten-year-old (with more questions than answers) appear quaint. The old ads for a night with Candy or Desire had to sell themselves with a simple stage name and tame offers of company in black text on newsprint. In the era of digital information, before readers view any ads hosted on thebackpages.com they are asked to agree with a disclaimer:

> *This section contains sexual content, including pictorial nudity and adult language. It is to be accessed only by persons who are 18 years of age or older (and is not considered to be a minor in his/her state of residence) and who live in a community or local jurisdiction where nude pictures and explicit adult materials are not prohibited by law. By accessing this website, you are representing to us that you meet the above qualifications. A false representation may be a criminal offence.*
>
> *I confirm and represent that I am 18 years of age or older (and am not considered to be a minor in my state of residence) and that I am not located in a community or local jurisdiction where nude pictures or explicit adult materials are prohibited by any law. I agree to report any illegal services or activities which violate the Terms of Use. I also agree to report suspected exploitation of minors and/or human trafficking to the appropriate authorities.*

The photos are mostly selfies in cheap, three-way bathroom mirrors. There was the odd professional shot, and my God I didn't know breasts could be that huge or bottoms that round or legs that long.

The captions were equally educational. I found out that I could contact an Upscale Italian Bella in a small town at least an hour away. There was "ALEYAH GiViN bEsT SeRvIcE iN tOWn XXX An 1 & MORE include." Aleyah not only played with her CAPS LocK A LOT, but she also used emoticons to her full advantage: red lips and a rain shower populates the text "BeSt MoUtH BeSt SkiLlZ".

There was Tiffany, Chinese Lisa, Rebecca from Aristocrat. There were a lot of hotties, and many promises of "girlz" "sweet" and "sexy", "juicy" and "tight." There were "big, natural boobs" and "Curvy Cougars" and there was Am3LIA who was "B3TT3R THAN H3R." (Subtle Am3LIA follows this boast with an up arrow then two pieces of cake with cherries on top). Massage offers were aplenty and Vikki offered help for "knotty man:" if you're knotty, Vikki will "Oil you up and Rub you down."

The Internet has helped many in the sex trade who once spent long nights waiting in the cold and with a simple, cheap ad comes better pay and the theory that the work is safer. Kate and the staff at CEASE take full advantage of the phone numbers on these online sites and they text and call the women with information on how to find help if they want to get out.

An awful lot say, "Thanks but no thanks."

A few say, "Fuck you."

And some say, "Yeah, I want out."

IIIII

On a recent March night I drove north on 95th Street, passed Norwood school then nearly ploughed into the back of a car that braked hard. Our headlights lit a woman who walked on the centre yellow line with a slight side step like she had ridden a horse too long. She looked back occasionally, her eyes impossible to read. The way she walked so purposefully in the centre of the road where she wouldn't get hit but where she had slowed down traffic, concerned me. I passed, paused, then uncharacteristically rolled down my window. "Can I help?"

Tears had tracked salt marks down her cheeks and a slight scar followed the top of her cheekbone along the curve of her eye then disappeared into her black, shoulder-length hair. She walked towards my door. "I need to get away from those guys." She looked behind us at the truck that wouldn't pass.

With surprising speed, she rounded my car's front grille to the passenger door and all I could think about was the interview I had just had with a former gang member who had worked these streets under the guise of streetwalker, and she had robbed hundreds of johns by telling them, "I have a place." Her words rattled my mind. "I robbed people alone, too. You know, just pull a shank."

No way, I couldn't do it. "I don't feel comfortable letting you in my car," I said as she raised her arm to open the passenger door. My blinkers were on and my heart sped. "But please, can I call someone?"

The hand that reached for the door handle dropped like a shooting star and she began to move again, this time on the dark sidewalk. I drove slowly along with my blinkers blazing and the line of cars behind me began to pass. I drew alongside her noticing her well-fitting jacket as she half-ran in platform shoes. "Please, can I call Crossroads?"

"Just forget it. No one cares a fuck about me." Her left arm waved like a magician's calling a rabbit from her black hat. *No one cares a fuck.* I can't forget it.

As I idled with tides of shame and uncertainty crashing about me, she turned and yelled, "Fine, call the cops." Or did she say, "Don't call the cops"? I didn't know what to do except drive steadily beside her. I was pulling ahead to ease around some parked cars when I saw in my rear view mirror her acid washed jeans flare white in the headlights as they left the sidewalk and climbed into the cab of a truck. *No one cares a fuck about me.* It was a boxy front grille and older-model lights. The truck passed and I saw only my car reflected in tinted windows.

16

Penis Slash and
Other Lessons

THE DAY I HAD ANTICIPATED and dreaded for five years finally arrived and so we stood out in morning rain that smelled of frost and waved goodbye. Madi's nose was a flat triangle pressed in the centre of the greasy window of a yellow bus driven by a stranger and as she waved we hid our anxiety behind smiles that were too broad and voices that were especially loud.

We comforted ourselves with the knowledge that we had prepared her as best we could for this first day of school. We had warned her of Stranger Danger and spoken of privacy and modesty and how friends don't keep secrets. I had told her of words that could get her in trouble if spoken out loud and she had practised reciting her home address, her phone number, her full name— I stopped at her Social Insurance Number.

That afternoon we returned to the same stop and waited as the bus braked and kids dribbled out. Our baby reached the top step and on seeing us she grinned, leapt to the curb, raced to her dad and with the dexterity of a martial artist landed a karate chop squarely to Mat's groin.

"Penis slash!" She shrieked with the kind of mischievous glee reserved for the best kind of phone pranks and we stood still as she ran for home. This is what she had learned in kindergarten?

||||||

With school came the addition of school friends. Raina lived down the street and was Madi's first friend to come home with her from the bus stop, had a lazy eye that sometimes went rogue checking out the house, the table set for dinner, the piano music, while her other eye focused on me and her request to stay for supper. I often said yes because she was the kind of kid I wanted to feed. "This is so good!" "Can I have more?" "What did you put in this?" She gushed as my kids eyed their plates like I had served them dysentery. When she finished, she would take her plate to the counter without being asked.

The first time we met her mom, she had pink streaked hair and wore an oversized hoodie over her oversized body. It was mid-October and she had only just realized that Raina was old enough for school.

We don't see much of their family, but they joined us for my birthday celebration, a foot-stomping, chaotic dance party with a bluegrass band complete with fiddler, bass and guitar set up in the living room where at least twenty-seven children went wild until midnight. As they left, Raina's mom thanked us for the invite. "It's so nice to be able to come to a party with our kids," she said, "and not have to leave when someone starts doing coke."

They weren't political or religious, nor were they really social. Raina went to church with her grandma and watched TV with her mom and cheered for her dad as he played video games. At our place she generally ran around in my heels, played pretend, or listened to the music of Katy Perry loud. She used "fuck" a lot.

"Fair enough, but in our house it isn't, okay?" I would say trying not to smile.

She tried, she really did try to not say it, but it came out at odd times. Friends from down the street had walked over and a half-dozen kids were racing to get their shoes on to walk the two blocks to the playground. Everyone except Raina was ready and waiting in the backyard when she popped her head from the kitchen and yelled, "Can someone help me find my fucking shoe?"

||||||

Raina is one of roughly one-third of local kids who goes to the neighbourhood public school with Madi. Both the Catholic and public school boards operate in an open-boundary system that allows for substantial parent choice. We could have sent Madi to any school in the city and there were many competing for our enrolment offering specialized programs focusing on arts, sports, languages, or appealing to specific cultural groups or religions. For us, the decision came down to two beliefs: we value strong community schools that require families in the neighbourhood to support it with their kids. Further, we see the benefit of having our kids' school friends also be their neighbourhood friends; besides keeping our driving for play-dates down to a minimum, it means that the significant parts of our lives all happen in close proximity and increases the potential of building ties to our neighbours.

Our decision was eased by Mat's experience in the school system since he had worked in the inner city junior highs around our home and knew what a fantastic staff and supportive environment these schools had for their students, and that included prekindergarten and full-day kindergarten where our children excelled.

||||||

Before the kids were strong enough on their bikes to cycle the eight blocks to school, when Lily started half-day prekindergarten, Madi would ride the yellow bus home and I drove the kids there. On the streets that lead north to school, the boulevard trees created a canopy that opened up at the fairly blank block of field surrounding the red brick building. The playground had been updated from the green, treated wood structures of my school days. However, sections of wood were beginning to lift on some of the platforms and most of the wooden steps hosted deep grooves filled with memories of thousands of frantic, frenetic steps.

The parent advisory council worked hard to raise funds for a new playground, and Mat played various roles, one of his least favourites being the lead on the Mom's Pantry catalogue fundraiser where mostly teachers purchased spices and frozen food. The council parents have worked casinos and organized silent auctions where, again, mostly teachers, mostly out of pity, bid for the odd assortment of goods on offer. There a couple of long-time volunteers who we see often in the community and whose kids long ago graduated from grade six, however, raising the funds has been hampered by the lack of available helping hands. In fact, the number of parents actively involved in the council can be counted on one hand and when new parents do show up for meetings it is usually because they misread or misunderstood the invitation their kid brought home, believing the meeting to be their parent-teacher conference appointment. These parents usually sit politely through the meeting and then never come again.

The playground's backdrop is a three-storey, flat-roofed school which squats eight blocks from our house, a fifteen-minute fast walk and forty-minute marathon with any child younger than six. Most mornings we would drive our van there in about two-and-a-half minutes, rolling past straggling groups of children. The three brothers who would pretend to smoke were usually later than we were. We arrived around the same time as one of my favourite kids whose mom walked to school in slippers and, depending on the weather, a lot of swaths of fabric from her home country in East Africa. When I first introduced myself I think she actually giggled at my pink hat crocheted in such a way that close-up it appeared like a web of nipples hugging my head. As I hustled the girls into school, we were usually right behind the boy in Lily's class whose dad dropped him off in a taxi (what I would have given to be driven to school in a taxi!). I was almost always much later than the little girl with two very organized moms who we frequently chatted with at the playground and farmer's market.

Lit by lamps and sunlight, Lily's prekindergarten class had a huge smart board that overlooked their circle time and centre time that rotated between the playhouse, paint station, and sand table. They started the day at the book nook as their graduate-level early education teacher and teacher's aide helped the fourteen three- and four-year-olds trace the dotted lines of their names next to grainy, coloured photos of themselves.

I was usually too late to catch most of the parents outside, but one warm winter's day I left and two moms stood against the wall chatting.

"You know this school has, like, sixty-nine percent mentally ill kids?"

"No way!" the other said. "Though I guess that makes sense."

I was confused. How could anyone know the number of mentally ill kids in a school? Numbers attempting to label the dysfunction at our school continued to crop up. Another parent lowered her voice as we waited in the halls for early release day and whispered, "This school is rough. Eighty-nine percent of kids have special needs."

I asked the school principal at the time what the actual stat was that people seemed to be quoting differently. Of the over four hundred students at the school, ninety-seven percent were what the school board deems socially vulnerable: meaning a lot of statistical factors put them at risk of not performing their best at school. These risk factors include low education level of parents, high government support received by families, new immigration status, English as a second language, single-parent families, low income, low mobility, parent tenancy and unemployment.

The public school board responded to the risk factors with resources in the form of teachers' aides, family counsellors, coaches, and occupational therapists. Wrapped around Delton were supports from a dozen other non-profit partners that provided snacks, lunches, mentors, and clubs. Field trips were extremely affordable and school supplies were free, many thanks to the parent council which, Mat discovered, once you join is hard to leave. The classrooms were filled with a kaleidoscope of cultures. In just one grade six class of eighteen, children were from Somalia, Cuba, Jamaica, Korea, the Philippines, and several First Nations. Madi was one of two blond kids in her class and one of a few who spoke only one language.

"Is this stat something I should be concerned about for my kids' sake?" I asked the principal.

The one negative she could suggest was that our kids may be exposed to curse words a little earlier than in other parts of the city. Like Madi's one friend whose "dad is a jerk because he doesn't call or send gifts on her birthdays." Or the one mom who tells her ex on the phone that he is a "goddamn fucking liar" and he is "going to fucking pay" as she pulls her three children into school. There were also the two seven-year-old girls in Madi's class who called one boy, "a frickin' ashhill" as they filed off the bus but this is the stuff that is in most schools, is it not?

What impacts the kids most is the transitory life of many of their peers. Of the almost four hundred students in the school in Madi's grade three year, almost half were new in September. Over the course of the year, another quarter revolved anew. This kind of transience, as families move in and out of transitional rental places, or children go in and out of government care, sets students back significantly. Sadly, these aren't the students Madi is most likely to connect with because they move all the time.

||||||

Raina would eventually move too, but in the three years they were in school together, they had a complicated relationship. Madi came home one day in grade two, wearing her school T-shirt which read on the back: "We do second chances/ We apologize/ We forgive/ We respect each other/ We keep our promises/ We never give up/ We encourage one another/ We laugh often / We belong...We are a family."

"Raina called me a loser today on the bus," she said.

"Why'd she say that?"

"Cuz she wanted me to say the 'f' word too."

"What did you do?"

"I just looked out the window."

"Do you think you're a loser?" I asked.

"No." She shrugged. "No, I'm not."

17

Aboriginal Dance

"I'M SCARED of doing Aboriginal dance at the winter concert,"
Madi said one afternoon in the beginning of December. I was chopping
veggies for a pot of chilli and she was searching for a snack to ruin her
dinner.

"You're performing at the winter show?" I asked, surprised.

"Yes, but I don't want to." She had joined the dance group at the
beginning of her second-grade year and when I asked why, she shrugged
and said it was fun. But performing in front of the whole school was a
different commitment than missing out on some freezing recesses over
the lunch hour.

"Why don't you want to perform? You like the dancing, right?"

"I have to jump around like this," she said, hopping back and forth
from one foot to another, strands of her white-blond hair stuck to her
lips. She was worried someone might make fun of her.

I let the conversation about dance die until later that night. As I
prepared a plate of crackers and meat for her bedtime snack, the CBC
newsreader calmly informed us that Nelson Mandela had died. He was 95.

"Who died?" she asked as she chomped her rice crackers like a fresh
piece of bubble gum.

She had started to notice the news and I hesitated, as I always did when she repeated some clip she had heard from the speakers in the back of the van: "Mom, did you hear a mom killed her kid? Mom, did you know there was an earthquake and the water is making people so sick they die? Mom, did you know a truck ran into a restaurant? Oh yeah, and a guy jumped off a building! He died."

"It was a South African man named Nelson Mandela who changed the government there," I said. "He was in jail for as many years as I've been alive."

"Was he a bad guy?"

"No. He didn't agree with what his government said about white and black people."

She stopped chomping and waited for me to go on. "The government separated the different colours and cultures and tried to make people believe that white people were better than blacks." There was an itching sensation at the back of my neck and a twisting in my gut.

She began chewing again, though her cream-pink jaw moved more slowly on the pickles. Their scent filled the space between us with vinegar. "I hate governments," she pronounced.

"Honey, governments are different country to country. It's not exactly fair to say you simply hate governments."

"What about our government?"

"We vote for them every few years, so we have a lot more power to change the way they treat people." But I knew I couldn't honestly stop there so I went on to tell a history she had yet to learn in school, and which I didn't learn until university. A history filled with promises that weren't kept and friendships that were broken. It was about bullying and stealing and lying. When I got to residential schools, she said, "Like the kids in *Despicable Me*?"

"That was an orphanage. These kids' parents weren't dead and didn't necessarily want them to go away to school." I went on to list the injustices: the kids couldn't speak their own language. They learned a different religion. Sometimes they were beaten so that they wouldn't fight back. And the kids couldn't play their drums. Or go to powwow. Or dance.

Madi was seven, the age when many children on reserve would have been told to "run into the bush" to escape the police tasked with collecting them for the school year. If this helpful, creative kid with soft skin and trusting eyes was forcibly removed from my life—because of her colour, because of my choice of religion, because of Mat's work, because of our roasted rabbit for breakfast and bannock for lunch—I don't know how I would move on.

"I know you don't want to perform for the school, Madi, and it's okay to feel embarrassed about doing something different in front of people," I said. "It's up to you."

||||||

When I was at school, we didn't have Aboriginal dance class and there were only two kids that I remember who looked Indigenous in my grade school set in the midst of Blackfoot territory. One was a girl whose long skirts and braids inspired by her earnest Christian community were defied by her quick tongue and wit. She was popular in that way strongly religious kids who don't get too preachy often are: they are liked, but not always included in after-school activities. She was a leader and regularly stepped up for student councils and peer support.

The other was a boy who could hit a baseball like the pros did on TV. He was the funny guy at the back of the class and he had many friends who drank together at bush parties. His last name changed in elementary school, from one that reflected the natural world to the Irish name of his foster parents. I noticed him on my first day as a new kid at the elementary school. He too was playing by himself in the shade at the back of the school, but what stood out for me were his braids.

When I go back to the pictures in my yearbook of his graduating class, about sixty students pose on the bleachers in satin gowns and shimmering ties and he stands at the back, one of the tallest in the class, smiling in his tux with short, spiky hair. The next time I would meet him he was in the line-up at the soup kitchen where I was working that night. We exchanged news of the past few years, careful to pretend nothing was weird about our current roles.

Five years later, I saw him again as the sky cleared its throat and coughed bits of spray threatening the usual late afternoon prairie thunderstorm. I hurried to strap the kids into their seats, and as I rounded the van to the driver's side, I spotted him walking down the alley. The veins in his long, skinny arms stretched like earthworms struggling for breath and ended in balled fists gripping black bags of bottles. His gait was slow, broken, cautious. His eyes were the vacant moons of a cheap high that didn't flick with any awareness of me and I looked down to appear unaware of him. That day in another alley behind our elementary school flashed behind my downcast eyes.

I kept my eyes down as I got in the van and waited for him to pass. With my forehead on the steering wheel, I tried to work through my options: I didn't want to get involved because I didn't want him to ask me for money, but I hadn't even given him a chance to ask! By the time I had worked out what was worse—the shame of not acknowledging him or the fear of setting boundaries—I had stepped out of the van, the rain was coming down, and he had disappeared.

▥

Two days before the concert, Madi got home from school and announced, "I made a big mistake, Mommy." As she kicked off her snow boots at the back entry then dropped her ski jacket in the middle of the kitchen floor, she said, "I practised Aboriginal dance and it was amazing."

She had been given a scarf to use in the girls' fancy dance and the waving fabric gave her sudden inspiration. For the rest of the night, she made Mat make drum beats on the guitar while she practised the step that bounced her around the room. Around the room, too, Lily practised her prekindergarten Diwali song involving hand movements that she explained to be "screwing in a light bulb." The concert celebrated holidays around the world with the requisite Hanukkah and snowman songs, hand bells and ukulele choir, performed for a packed gym filled with brown, white, pink, black and tanned people.

That night, I stood nervously in the centre aisle with my camera ready. An Ethiopian mother and Indian father waited for the act to start too. The dance troupe was scheduled near the end of the long evening and thin air had absorbed the worst smells in the room: stale cigarette smoke and cheap cologne.

Then seven kids stepped onstage single file. From the tinny, tiny speakers came the sound of the drum that cued the kids. Their bouncing and fist pumping didn't always correspond with the beat or the call of the Cree singers and one much taller girl covered Madi in her shawl for most of the performance. I have no idea whether they nailed it. In fact, it probably wasn't close to correct, but as I snapped pictures I knew in my gut it was good.

18

We Are All
in This Together

ALBERTA AVENUE is home to three out of every five Aboriginal
people who live in Edmonton and just under half of them struggle below
the poverty line. In another brick building ten blocks away from the kids'
school, Bent Arrow Traditional Healing Centre leases the old Parkdale
elementary school, where Mat had worked with students in junior high.
Two years before Madi entered school, the public school board con-
solidated the city centre schools in part due to the old building's growing
maintenance costs, and in part due to pressure from burgeoning
classroom needs in the suburbs.

When I first met Bent Arrow's Executive Director, Cheryl Whiskeyjack,
I was a community member helping to coordinate a Safe Halloween
Party in their gym and grounds. Over one thousand people came out for
Halloween stories in the teepee, for wagon rides and a failed fireworks
display. The agency has regular soup and bannock lunches that are open
to everyone in the neighbourhood, as well as a long menu of services that
aim to introduce the Aboriginal worldview into social work. One of these
services is a program called Kahkiyaw (for short), meaning "all people,
especially traditional people, are related" in Cree. Initially, it was a pilot
project where the Indigenous agency worked alongside government

child welfare workers to support (mostly) Indigenous families in the centre of the city. I met Cheryl again while I was researching an essay on decolonizing the child welfare system. I wanted to understand how Kahkiyaw was reclaiming a system that had been one of the main vehicles—after residential schools—for cultural genocide. Our interview was at the Carrot Coffeehouse where the latte machine squealed and a volunteer cashier looked slightly panicked about counting out my change. We found a table tucked against the front window.

Cheryl is Ojibwa from northern Ontario and she grew up in a loving family. Her parents met at residential school and even named her after their favourite nun, Alberta, which is her middle name. Cheryl's husband, Elmer, grew up on the land of the Saddle Lake First Nation where his first chore of the day was always a rush. Shoes thrown on with his T-shirt askew, he raced outside in the dark to beat the magpies and hawks to his family's breakfast on the trap line. He works in the industry that serves the oil patch now and whenever the men in the lunchroom titter about the falling oil prices and the corresponding price of their shares, he shrugs. He has lived on rabbit trapped in the forest and he knows he can do it again.

"I tease my husband when he gets his treaty money," said Cheryl. "Five bucks from the government. It's the price of this latte." But it's more than that, we both know. Treaty Day marks an agreement signed by two equal parties and on-reserve Mounties stand at attention in polished boots and ceremonial red serge as the Queen's guard distributes the funds as outlined in the treaties to all band members.

"And you, are you treaty?" I asked.

"No," she said. Her band never signed one. "But you are."

You are. The words echoed like an aftershock. *You are.*

When I asked Cheryl about the path to establishing true reconciliation after the years of failed promises, she told me about a vision they had when they approached the elders with their idea for the Kahkiyaw program. Bent Arrow leaders had asked the elder, "How can we work differently with our families?" The vision they were given was of a Sundance: a ceremony that was illegal to perform for half a century.

"The sundancer puts themselves in a position of sacrifice for four days and four nights," Cheryl explained. "No drinking. No eating. They do sweats, and they dance from sun up to sun down. They pray all the time, focusing entirely on the colourful flags that hang on the Tree of Life at the centre of the circle. The pieces of fabric represent hundreds of different prayers of the people. The sundancer is dancing for each person; that he will get his answer. They are dancing for you, for me, for her, for my grandma, for my son, for your son. They are doing it for everyone but themselves.

"We need to see our families as sundancers. A sundancer is put in a place of honour because they are sacrificing so much for people they don't know and our families are putting themselves in a place to change; they are sacrificing for their children, their families, and their community. And, if we treated them as if they were in a position of honour, then the whole way we approach working with them certainly would be different."

Every Sundance also has an oskapew, a sacred helper, who supports the sundancer by keeping her fire lit and ensuring there are enough blankets and chopped wood. The helper does whatever the dancer needs so that the she can focus. "That is our job as practitioners," said Cheryl, "to support our families in the work they are doing. Not to tell them what to do, but to support them in the work *they* are doing."

Kahkiyaw. We are all in this together.

19

A Salmon's
in the Koi Pond

FOR A WHILE after Lily was born, I was home all day, every day with two kids under the age of three and my restless mind circled at the speed of light vaulting me spastically between completely disparate tasks. When Mat arrived home from work, I would assail him with the documents I had drafted: preliminary drawings for an entire second floor addition heated by passive solar energy and topped by a greenhouse sunroom, an Excel sheet of brands and prices of strollers, a financial plan built from the advice of the library's entire investment section.

My children seemed unaware of the frenetic energy bubbling in my heart that completely belied my setting. I felt like a spawning salmon caught in the central pond of a Japanese garden. Because I am slightly more reflective than a salmon I could recognize the beauty and blessing of my surroundings (I mean, how many women in North America get twelve months of paid maternity leave?). Because I am smarter than a salmon, I could recognize that this was just a season in my life. Because I am an animal like a salmon, however, I thrashed and struggled in that pond to do what I needed to do.

Unlike that salmon, I am able to spawn anywhere and Ali was conceived two years later despite all the emotional discomfort which I eventually converted to energy and turned like a laser beam on making household products from scratch. I have always had a DIY streak in me, but when the local newspaper, *The Rat Creek Press*, approached me about writing a column, I pitched that I could write about the truth and fiction in making products from scratch. The idea was that I would test and review the recipes that dripped with eco-boosterism but so often in reality were rife with basic problems (for example, olive oil does not remove lice. Picking nits off your head does). I called the column "An Avenue Homesteader" to ride the urban farming fad and tap into my off-the-grid hippy side and the column spun off into a blog, which I maintained for a record eighteen months.

I started out with fairly easy projects like making Irish Cream and pancake mix, then moved on to more complicated recipes like body butter, soap bars, and laundry detergent. I designed my own spray bottles so that all the cleaning solution recipes were written on them like a salad dressing cruet: basic (water, vinegar and a little soap), super (add more vinegar and soap), mould-busting (add Borax: a white powder in a green box in the laundry aisle). For a time, I was so thrilled with my spray bottles I considered getting a table at the Alberta Avenue farmer's market to sell DIY Cleaning Supplies Starter Kits.

I hit some rough patches with Mat. For one week, I experimented with replacing our coffee intake with dandelion tea, tenderly harvesting the roots of the foot-wide plants that propagated in our alley and lawn. After scrubbing the soil and silt off, I roasted the roots in the oven until they dried and curled like a hard fungus, then using our bladed coffee grinder I ground the bejesus out of them—possibly not the first of a number of mistakes. While the roots were more powder than ground, into the French press they went, chased by hot water. Stir. Plunge. Pour. Drink. Mat was polite enough to not spit it out, though I would not have blamed him if he had. He later asked if it was possible to just buy dandelion tea. Like tea bags in a box. He also wondered how he could get the root powder out of the crevices of the grinder blades.

I know he never loved the baby wipes I made. They were cheaper and with fewer chemicals and by-products than those from the crinkly, white packages in the store. Take a roll of paper towel, saw it in half to form two toilet-paper-sized rolls. Place this roll into a large container with the hole facing up. Add a mixture of water, castile soap, and oil, then close the lid. Next time the bottom requires it, pull the wipes from the centre and voila! Wipes for half the price. His concern was two-fold: first, often when you needed them most, they needed to be made. And two, I was not always good at getting the more expensive paper towel. In these instances, the paper disintegrated at the very time in the diaper change one needs it most. But it was so cheap and they were homemade, which surely helped me overlook some of the other reasons one might have for choosing a product.

Mat's brain just is not wired for such deals. Our homemade wine, for instance, I drank for far longer than he could stomach it. "It costs three dollars a bottle, Mat!"

"Okay, but can you not see that the deal has completely changed your taste buds? It has physiologically changed how you experience this wine." And it's true; the deal and the fact that it was homemade changed how I prioritized success so that instead of flavour being at the top of my checklist, it had mysteriously taken third or fourth place.

My passion inadvertently drew him into its swirling vortex, like the Saturday he spent sawing and drilling in the fiercest spring snowstorm of the past fifty years. A previous owner had poured an expensive cement pad adjacent to our detached garage. After we moved in and in my haste to plant the entire property with edibles, I said to my neighbour over our three-foot fence that we might jack hammer the pad up. We did not need it. There was the garage for our car and it was one of the few places on the property with limitless access to the sun. My neighbour nearly choked on the candy he was eating. "Do you know how much that pad cost?" I had no idea. "Ten thousand dollars! They poured that and added the closing fence so that their truck wouldn't get stolen." While I may love grass and loam more than the previous owners, my fiscal sensibilities are also strong. Suddenly the cement pad was an asset and while it was not one that I wanted, perhaps another owner would.

That month I found a book that would change the trajectory of a weekend that Mat meant to spend inside with a nice cup of tea. Squinting through the huge snowflakes, he followed the instructions laid out in Mel Bartholomew's book *The NEW Square Foot Gardens* to build four raised garden beds. With about four hundred dollars and Mat's sweat equity, the ten-thousand dollar cement pad was restored to garden space.

One of our last projects for the blog also took place on that same back pad and Mat's Saturday was again hijacked, this time by my obsession to build a solar oven. I flew about pulling out random bits from the garage, a bike tire, an old window, an emergency blanket and wooden box, shouting over my shoulder at Mat, "I think you'll need your drill, hon!" He huffed, "I think I should write a blog about being married to a blogger."

If he had written that blog, he would have in equal measure celebrated and lamented my bread fanaticism. For quite a few months I refused to buy any kind of bread products and while I think my neighbours and friends appreciated it, the policy meant that when Mat went searching for bread to toast and there wasn't any, I would shout, "Just have to make it, babe!" He would silently make a pot of oatmeal.

The feat of that restless time, for me, was the discovery of a bread recipe that at its most basic was this:

6 cups of flour
1 tablespoon of yeast
1 teaspoon of salt
3 cups of water

I remember it as the formula $6 / (1 + 1) = 3$, though Mat says this math just confuses him more. About a year after I shared this recipe on the blog, I stood in the industrial kitchen of the community hall surrounded by nineteen people including four men, two women older than sixty, and every decade from the 1920s to 1960s. There was a woman who spoke Mandarin, a man from the Caribbean, and one fellow with crutches. Most of them wore aprons they had brought from home and a couple of them already had flour on their hands. Thanks to a two-hundred-and fifty-dollar small project grant from the city's revitalization initiative, and the donation of kitchen space by the League, participants paid five dollars each for the afternoon of bread-making, baking, and eating.

They paired up and with a large bowl between them made white bread, pizza crust, and cinnamon buns. They experimented by adding seeds, sugar, nuts, dried fruit, and herbs. I wanted people to see that the one recipe—with a little more or a little less flour depending on the purpose—could be used for any bread like pitas, buns, cinnamon twists, and baguettes. All were slight variations of the same theme. We ate well that afternoon and everyone left with some Ziploc bags of dough to cold-rise in their fridge.

After that successful, heady beginning, the one small grant funded six other workshops. Another columnist at the paper led the seed-starting workshop. Fifteen people made baby slings at the Carrot with sewing help from my sister-in-law. We learned from a neighbour how to graft fruit trees and plant square-foot gardens. Fifteen women gathered to make beauty products, one cheerfully endured the scalding power of lye on the skin for the sake of affordable beauty, and another twenty came to make cleaning products. No two groups were the same and many of the people I have never again seen in the community. Perhaps this is all that can be expected from community development work: comfort that there is company in the koi pond, and if one burns their bread they know how to make more.

20

Taking Over the Streets

THE BOY WAS SURVEYING every adult in the playground on a night when the mosquitoes were bad and it was unusually muggy for this dry prairie town. I overheard him talking about money so when he approached me and Drea I shook my head. "No, thanks, I'm not interested."

"Just, just five minutes of your time, please?" His voice was shaking and he tilted his head as though he might bury it in the ground at any moment.

"I'm not interested."

For a nervous guy he was awfully persistent. "Don't you want to hear about what I have to say?" I did not. "No, thank you."

A couple of nights later, Mat said, "I forgot to tell you about the most awkward kid at the park last night."

"I saw him too!"

"Did you take his survey?"

"No, I thought he was selling something."

"You didn't even give the kid a chance?"

"No..." I paused to show my contrition. "What was he selling?"

"He was trying to organize a festival."

Over the past ten years that the city has funded revitalization efforts, our community has hosted many festivals but the most well known is Kaleido, now organized almost entirely from the Carrot Coffeehouse.

The Carrot is a unique community hub and almost entirely volunteer-run. Hailed as a salvation by artists, stay-at-home parents and locals seeking a decent caffeinated beverage, it's also a critical meeting place. The local paper, arts groups, a food network, the knitting club, a book club, and the farmers' market's committee connect around kitschy tables—some donated, others bought for cheap at the thrift stores along the Avenue.

Its four-by-eight-foot stage hosts travelling bands, open mics and spoken word poetry. Each month a new visual artist speaks from the walls, and always one can buy birthday gifts from the glass cases that showcase local artisans' jewellery, leatherwork, and pottery.

When the Carrot first opened, Madi was just seven months old and we signed up to be baristas for the Tuesday night volunteer shift. We were paired with a man who lives across the alley from us who has been blind since birth and who made the majority of the espresso while Mat and I handled the cash and customer service.

A year later, Mat joined the Carrot's operations committee that like most committees has meetings that are too long and whose agenda items are important but minutiae all the same. They vacillate painfully over questions like: Should children's hot chocolate be served in a six- or eight-ounce cup? Should the bathrooms be cleaned every shift or just every night? Are the complaints about the muffins being dry true?

The macro questions that intimately affect the tone and culture of the space take up a huge chuck of discussion time too: What do we do when someone comes in high or drunk from the bar next door? How do we support the hard of hearing man who insists on doing sound at Saturday open mic nights? Exactly how do we diplomatically state the obvious— that parents must parent their kids when they are having three-hour-long coffee chats?

For my part, the weekly Friday Babes in Arms group was a buoy when my girls were small and I was the primary parent at home. They would scramble confidently onto a worn sofa tucked against a back wall while I ordered our drinks and bags of chips. Over the next hour moms and dads would swap inventories of the minutes we did and did not sleep. We conducted informal polls: how many held feces that day? Who tried to hide a pool of pee in the supermarket? Who ate cereal and milk three meals in a row? Laughing is better than crying and surely belonging is better than failing. Sharing a fully formed thought was recognized as overrated and we resigned ourselves to conversations that flowed like Morse code: *di dit dah dah dah STOP dit dah di dit STOP di di dit.*

In retirement, my dad has discovered the comforts of those couches too and every morning he walks with his book to the Carrot. Settling in by the large front bay window he reads and partially listens as the Arts on the Ave team plan the community's two biggest festivals: Kaleido in the fall and Deep Freeze in the new year. Occasionally, the Executive Director, Christy Morin, will finish a conversation with a sponsor or publicist and she will turn to Dad, with a "Doug, what did you think about that?"

Christy's experience living next to a drug house in part inspired Arts on the Ave. She finished high school in a tough inner city school after the administration decided to focus on music, drama and visual art. As a passionate drama student, she had seen the transformative power of the arts to change a culture so she gathered a small group of people in her living room and they discussed the question of what they could do to encourage people to visit and perhaps even move in to Alberta Avenue without fear.

The Alberta Avenue part of 118th Avenue runs between 82nd Street and 101st Street and is a short distance north from downtown. In the pre-war years, it was a significant business thoroughfare, but as the working class families moved to the suburbs after the second world war, the main street's smile was transformed into a gap-toothed sneer by absentee landlords, pawn shops, and vacant lots through the 1980s and

1990s. It cuts east-west through the centre of the four neighbourhoods of Norwood, Delton, Eastwood, and Parkdale. These encompass the communities that make up the area referred to as Alberta Avenue where the large majority of residents rent single, detached houses reaching the end of their lifespan.

For the last thirty years, the community battled the same branding problem Edmonton has faced on a national and international scale, meaning if people knew where Alberta Avenue was, it was safe to say they would ask you, "Why would you live *there*?"

There were many people who wanted to change that question and the small group of artists in Christy's living room would play a key role in beginning to shift the perception. The festivals grew because the right funding and people were there, but also because the festivals like those that Arts on the Ave built captured the best of our neighbourhood's creative people. Our musicians found a stage to play on alongside national bands, our visual artists were given galleries to showcase their work, our theatre directors found audiences to perform for.

Our children have internalized it all. We were at Popular Bakery ordering custard tarts when the Portuguese owner asked Madi, "What do you want to be when you grow up?"

"A balloon artist," she said without pause then hid her head when we all laughed in surprise. For Christmas that year, we bought her a balloon tying kit. She was five and made hats and dogs and swords for all her friends at every party for the next couple of months. She instructed the vibrating kids that they needed to form a line (they obliged) and they needed to be patient (they tried to oblige), then she worked the parents in the room for their spare change.

The Awkward Boy in the park had also caught the festival bug. "You need to say yes or no," he instructed Mat who agreed to do the survey. "So, do you say three dollars for a hot dog, pop, and chips? Yes or no?"

"I'd say, 'no', because that's too low. You need to make some money. I think you should charge five dollars."

"So you say 'no' to four dollars?"

"Yes, I say 'no'".

"But, you say 'yes' to five dollars."

"Yes." He marked Mat's responses in his lined notebook.

"Okay, I'm going to sell popcorn. Do you say 'yes' to a small bag of popcorn like this," he indicated with his hands a bag the size of a paperback book, "for one dollar?"

"Yes, I say 'yes'." Mat watched Lily as she chased some kid around the park and the crowds at the football stadium fifteen blocks away roared.

"Do you say 'yes' then to two dollars for a big bag of popcorn?"

"Yes," Mat said shifting.

"Okay, I'm going to sell pop too..." Awkward Boy, who wore baggy blue jeans and basketball shoes but otherwise did not look like he played any kind of sport, carefully wrote down 'yes' and 'no' as he went through a very long list of concession items, activities, and boundaries for a festival-style day. Just as Mat was about to quit the interview, the boy said, "Final thing, I want to have face painters. I'm thinking of charging five dollars for face painting."

"Now hang on. So I have to donate money for the kids to play the games. Your food prices are okay. I have to spend ten dollars to see the bands. And now, five dollars for face painting? This is becoming way too much for a family."

"It's really expensive because we're doing air brush face painting. So do you say yes to five dollars?"

"No, I've got three kids and that's fifteen dollars for them to get their face painted, so I say 'no'."

"Fine. What if it was three for five dollars?" Even at the end the boy's voice shook from nerves and finally he moved on to other parents in the Alberta Avenue Community League playground. Otherwise known as the Ship Park, the park is in the centre of the Kaleido activities. It sits next to the League gardens that hosts the Friday night outdoor movie and often a beer gardens or concert stage on Saturday. Every year the crowds walk past the metal equipment in the festival's kick-off lantern parade. With our homemade paper lanterns, we walk with our neighbours, costumed stilt walkers, clowns, and hula hoopers. With the Chinese gong at the front and djembe players at the back, the crowd finds a pace and moves along the Avenue, through the playground, past the food trucks and six-foot wide bonfires to a giant stage for the opening ceremonies.

At the main stage, a band starts their first song and the parade crowd's forward-motion shifts to up and down. Bouncing old people, young people, poor people, rich people find themselves apologizing for crushing each other's toes or kids, then laughing because we just cannot help ourselves. The festival is open to everyone for free.

Saturday and Sunday is a mad rush of discovery: Two roving actors paddle in a cardboard canoe hitched up around their hips; a creature wearing a gas mask and round goggles rappels from a roof; wall dancers dance perpendicular to the ground; a trombone choir playing Beatles tunes leaps without warning onto a balcony; sudden mobs of zombies dance to *Thriller* and scare my small children; a rock band plays inside the orthodox church; a jazz trio inspires a couple to spontaneously tango under a weeping birch.

Inside the Carrot the folkies play to crowds, half of them waiting patiently for their latte that will take about half an hour to get to by the feverish volunteers. Across the street the heavy beat of a Lindsey Stirling song plays from the Bedouin Beats main stage. The belly dance studio showcases hours of hip-waving womanhood to large crowds of people that include only a small number of videographers who film the free show for reasons other than art.

Plays for a back seat audience of three occur in moving cars in the back alleys. One can learn to hula-hoop in the middle of the street, or buy a felted fox pillow made from recycled wool sweaters, or eat buffalo burgers with vegan poutine. Occasionally even nature participates. One night after Delhi to Dublin had played their fusion of wild Irish fiddle with a booming Indian beat and the parking lot had been filled with people from all over the city who had forgotten to be self-conscious for just an hour or so, Mat and I started walking home with the buzz of music still in our ears. Mat took my arm. "Look up," he said.

Mine joined a collective cry from up and down the street that rose
to meet the shifting lights in the sky. The colour of well-fertilized grass,
the Northern Lights danced in undulating, random patterns, snaking
north then south; light and dark smoked and curled around one another
completely oblivious they had an audience who craned their necks then
lay down on the closed road to breathe it in.

21

Predators Invade

MY GREAT-GRANDFATHER used to mail me short letters in a wavering hand on memo pad paper from his seniors' home in Toronto. They were simple letters from a man who had learned to write later in life. He would describe his supper or his roommate. However, the one I most keenly remember, because we howled with the laughter of children who presume their superiors' senility, was a simple list of trees. There was no starting "Dear" or final "Love." Just a very long list that included American oaks and maples. I can only suppose they were trees whose boughs scratched at his window during heavy Eastern storms and swished coolly above him during humid naps on the grounds. They were trees that had outlived my great-grandma and they would soon outlive him.

Time has brought some insight into all that went unspoken in his letters. Trees mark and measure a great deal of the last hundred years in Alberta Avenue, whose boulevards were planted with elm trees by forward thinking city workers and which now stretch thirty feet tall. In a number of front yards tall pines stretch twice the height of the two-storey houses and a hundred times taller than they were when, as Arbour Day seedlings, children of the 1970s received them at school then planted them in spots too close to foundations.

Many of the most run-down properties have at least a crabapple tree or the remains of a fifty-year-old caragana hedge that captures every Oh Henry wrapper, Doritos bag, and failed lotto card dropped on the sidewalk, but that hints at previous care. Even the truly dejected properties are transformed in spring by resilient, low-maintenance lilacs whose early blooms pop purple and unleash a scent with a special kind of power in our winter city: walkers who for months hurried along the sidewalks navigating ice and poorly shovelled sections with their heads down, suddenly look up, stop, then turn towards a stranger's home and inhale so deeply that their chests strain the buttons on their soon-to-be-stored parkas. Like heat on ice, the lilac scent softens our hearts and frees our tongues. It's a small window of time—two weeks, maybe three at most—where perfect strangers can be found chatting then laughing wildly at one another's lame jokes. They can be heard saying over and over like rogue cuckoo birds, "What a lovely day."

Every year once the snow melts and the lilacs finish their bloom, my husband and I stand back across the street to fully appreciate the egregious state of our front yard, with its lawn of sheared-off aggressive weeds shaded by three trees. One is a lilac bush, sculpted into a tree form under which the creeping lilies-of-the-valley catch most of the yellowed Canadian Tire flyers and 7-Eleven tostada boxes the wind blows in. Its two trunks are twisted, gnarled like lizard skin built to withstand bitter weather that fearlessly plunges deeper than the absurdly chilly minus thirty degrees celsius.

The yard is also shaded by a forever-green cedar, once trained into an ellipse, or perhaps a bubble-font exclamation point. Because of our negligence its style is shifting to a more asymmetrical business at the bottom, party at the top. With its sides shaved as high up as Mat can reach with the shears and its top overgrown, it's more punk rock than Buddhist monk.

The third tree is a mountain ash positioned centre front; it grows taller every year. Yes, I know that all trees (besides my ficus, which has lived half-dead for the past five years in my living room) tend to do what many describe as grow taller, but this mountain ash with mandarin colour berries and Halloween shades in the fall, really grows. We have two in the back, both with red berries and fall colour, that have remained compact and we trim them only when their berries grow so heavy with snow that they christen our six-foot friends' heads with ice powder. The front mountain ash should have been trimmed years ago before it passed the peak of our roofline but now it's well past Mat's reach and we have a major problem with what designers call scale.

From our second floor window we watch the birds in this tree. I have seen young house sparrows gain confidence for flight by leaping from heights that would generally be considered suicide. As I watch the babies jump, then catch the air, then flutter, then fall, then catch the air again, I feel that same feeling one has passing a car crash.

One spring, in what I can only imagine as pure diligence on their part or poor maintenance on ours, the birds pushed aside a section of fascia at the roof's highest peak. Having opened the door, they moved right in and as most animals are prone to do when finding themselves warm, dry, and sheltered from prying eyes, promptly had babies.

The chirping of those chicks offered us a new soundtrack as we creaked back and forth on the porch swing drunk with the scent of spring. At first it was novel and we marvelled at it. As the sound increased and lilac smell decreased, the chicks were tolerated. At some point in time, however, I snapped and decided they needed to move or die and I turned up the spray nozzle's water pressure hoping to blast the damn chicks away only to discover the water hose barely reached the front and that it's hard to aim accurately when you are spraying through the new growth of a four-metre wide mountain ash. I was pelted by winter-dried berries and ricocheting droplets of water.

Despite wanting to discourage chicks noisily serenading me from the fascia, that summer I wanted to encourage more birds in the yard. Most of my gardening books were telling me that birds are an important part of the urban landscape, that they are critical for natural control of the critters gardeners like to hate: slugs, aphids, ants. Without further research, I strung up a birdfeeder in the back yard mountain ash and within hours, to my delight and no small amount of pride at my incredible largesse in response to the birds' plight of assumed starvation (because the mountain ash berries surely didn't provide the nutrients millet could), I sat on my deck and heard bird song.

Not many days later, I opened my eyes and saw these creatures as bullies. "You know, you can legally kill the babies," said the operator on the other end of my call with a city bird hotline after I described the flocks in my attic.

"I didn't know that," I said although I had, in fact, limply tried with my water nozzle. The legality of killing such birds had never occurred to me. I didn't know that one would want to kill the creatures besides when they were annoying to listen to while spending leisure time on one's front porch.

"Yes, in Alberta it's legal to kill these birds. House sparrows are an invasive species and the fewer babies, the fewer of them." He went on to tell me about how his group builds, places and maintains mountain blue bird nesting boxes across kilometres of walking trail. The mountain blue bird is slightly smaller than the house sparrow and distinguished by the males' black front bib. "I've come upon nests where the eggs were raided and the mother blue bird has been killed, her eyes pecked out, or mauled, leaving her with a major head or chest injury. We've come upon nests where the house sparrow has made her nest on top of the dead body of the blue bird. These are vicious birds. They are invaders, conquerors and if we don't stop them, nature sure won't."

That day I took down the feeder that allowed the sparrows to procreate with full bellies and no fear of future want. We then tightened up the fascia so the birds couldn't break in to procreate in the shelter and heat.

As I looked about with more educated eyes, I saw predators all around me. One afternoon we watched a crow sweep from the sky to skewer a magpie to death with its beak. There were falcons, magpies, blue jays and ravens loitering in all the best trees on the block.

Only twice have I seen songbirds in our back yard: a lone finch and two red-breasted mezzo-sopranos that provided a lovely change from the house sparrows' "I've-been-drinking-for-hours-and-finally-feel-brave-enough-to-get-up-and-sing-this-Frank-Sinatra-song." Despite the lack of a native bird soundtrack, the trees continue to grow and provide creatures a home. If my great-grandfather were still alive I would write him a letter.

Dear Great-Grandpa,

Mountain Ash (Winter Colour)
Honeyberry Bush (Food)
Chokecherry (Fall Colour)
Columnar Cedar (Privacy)
Columnar Aspen (Music)
Highland Cranberries (Food/Privacy)
Hops (Shade)
Explorer Rose (June Colour)
Juliet Choke Cherry (Food)
September Ruby Apple (Food/ Shade)
Saskatoon Berry Bush (Food)
Raspberries (Food)
Lilac (Scent/Spring Colour)
Weeping Caragana (Winter Interest)
Pembina Plum (Food/Privacy)
Manitoba Maple (Seedlings/Annoying)

Love,
Carissa

22

Privacy's Found
in the Basement

OUR FAMILY'S SLEEPING ARRANGEMENT has generally left everyone tired. In our storey-and-a-half bungalow, two bedrooms are nestled in the joists of the house reachable by a steep set of fir-topped stairs. Over the course of three pregnancies I cursed these stairs as I traversed the narrow treads to the washroom in the middle of the night.

By that time, I was also generally cursing the children as one or two and later even all three made the short trek from their shared room to our bed. Over time, Mat and I tired of sleeping at the edges of our double bed, rail straight, trying to escape the small elbows and feet, so we bought a foam king-sized mattress that fit into our room. Literally. It was wall-to-wall bed leaving no one at risk of falling off the edge. However, after a time we changed our minds again. Even with a king-size, our blankets were incrementally removed from our bodies by rolling children and we realized that no matter how much room we had, our warm bodies were nectar feeding their hunger for touch. We would wake up with our cheeks pressed against the wall, a child's drool-encrusted cheek stuck to our back and a yawning canyon space in the centre.

In a fit inspired by a sleep-deprived brain, Mat took a serrated bread knife to the thick foam mattress and sawed it back down to the size of a double. Next to the bed we put kids'-sized mats as a concession: "If you must come in, you may sleep on the floor." They grumbled at our instructions, but the sleep solution worked until a strange series of events made us realize perhaps it was time for more privacy.

▌▌▌▌▌

I was in my mid-thirties and of average weight when I learned my genetics had stamped my heart with a handicap: my cardiovascular system collects cholesterol like a magpie gathers silver spoons. My doctor and I discussed my options to reduce the risk factors of a major heart attack. "Exercise will reduce your chance of a heart attack by about the same amount as statins, the most common type of cholesterol medication."

I wasn't that keen to exercise until she added, "You should know that when statins are started in a patient's thirties, there is some concern about the long-term impact on the brain."

Threat of heart attack or threat of early onset dementia. Between those two fearsome options, I decided I probably should choose exercise.

"How much exercise?" I asked.

"One hundred and fifty minutes a week," my doctor said.

Twenty-two minutes a day was the length of a SpongeBob episode. Fuck. "That long?"

I have had success with exercise regimes that varied between the Fail, Near Fail, and Moderate Suck ranges. I did the Wii Fit for a while, I lift a lot of kids, but I can't seem to build running or the gym or even belly dance classes into my day. But then again, I didn't have the doctor wielding sticks of "Heart Attack" or "Triple By-Pass at Forty." So I did what every thinking person does in the age of social networks, I asked my friends on Facebook what kind of devices they used to get fit. It was by far one of my most popular and commented upon status updates.

Pedometers and fitness apps, mini-steppers, ellipticals.

So began the Preparation phase. This is the phase that I do best (after what the theorists call "pre-contemplation," which means exactly what it sounds like: you aren't even thinking about it). For me, Preparation generally equates to making purchases, so I bought a mini-stepper that advertised how small and mobile it was. The models looked very happy to be on their modified hamster wheel that twisted slightly to work the glutes and came with stretchy tubes that promised to build my arms.

I downloaded a fitness app that required me to input every food item that entered my mouth and came with a convenient scanning feature. On any product that had a bar code, my phone could scan its nutritional information so I spent a week wildly scanning the products in my fridge and snack cupboards. This didn't help me when I made my own food and many nights of chicken stew with a cauliflower side went by without input. Overall, the absence of this information left me feeling great as the app told me I had four hundred calories remaining at the end of each day. Seeing my daily caloric intake so low made me feel great largesse towards myself. Despite that I knew—I knew!—the math was wrong, it afforded me a glass of wine or bowl of chips at the end of the day.

The Preparation phase also led me to my favourite local bra shop downtown where I bought not one but two sports bras. One had a dozen front hooks, was metallic purple and when I put it on made me feel like Wonder Woman with two large pancakes on my chest. Sometimes, it actually made me feel like exercising.

Finally, I ordered a Fitbit online. Mat's question, "Don't you think it's time you just started to exercise?" hung in the air as I clicked Buy. When the tiny pedometer arrived, it fit snuggly and inconspicuously in my cleavage whose bounce I secretly hoped would trick the counter into added extra steps.

The Fitbitch, as I came to call my codependent friend, led me to the "Action" phase of change. It talked to my phone and sent me weekly alerts about how many stairs I had climbed and how far I had fallen short on my 10,000 step goal. I rose to the challenge and walked to prove the damn mini-screen wrong, and when I did it rewarded me with scrolling messages. "Awesome job, Carissa." And "You can do it."

The tiny gadget could also track my sleep. It slipped into a wristband and tracked my nightly movements that reportedly established my sleep state: Asleep, Restless, Awake. It was also a useful timer.

Mat's a musician and one night he had a show after which we stayed up late talking, drinking wine, reviewing the performance. By two AM, we fell into bed and each other.

After I had caught my breath, I laughed. "How long did that take?"

I checked my pedometer's timer and read out the minutes and seconds.

"That is so, so not sexy," he groaned, forgetting that we had both lost the need to be long ago.

A small, high voice cut through our cocoon of blankets.

"Daddy?" we froze. "Did you say a bad word?"

Shit. If she had heard him say "sexy" what else had she heard? Shaking with silent laughter and small twinges of horror, we resolved that night that it was time to get ourselves our own room.

||||||

We bought our house before we had kids and it felt huge at the time. After Alistair was born, however, we began the search for a new house with a third bedroom and another bathroom. Our side of 118th Avenue still had very few larger homes as the lots are small at thirty-three feet across. Alberta Avenue also has very few newer homes and Mat had let himself start dreaming about an electrical panel from which new cables and wires streamed in predictable fashions and were installed by ticketed professionals. We expanded our property search to communities a little farther from the centre, keeping it in the limits of the 1950s boundaries of the city. After a few months, we found a home in a community called Montrose which butted up against a bluff beyond which thousands of vehicles travelled on Yellowhead Trail. A former lotto Dream Home, the owners had bought the place from the lottery winner, with furniture, paintings and decor all included. To us it was virtually new (twenty-five years) and was a massive 1,800 square feet and in its undeveloped basement was the Holy Grail of electrical panels. The yard was also suburban-style huge at almost three times the size of ours, and it had fruit trees, perennials, and a well-tilled veggie garden. It was going to cost us double the selling price of our home, an astronomical amount in the eyes of a writer and mid-level social worker-type. We hoped that we might keep our Alberta Avenue house and rent it, but before the bank would agree to that plan it needed to see the place first.

The man they sent arrived promptly at ten on a Tuesday morning. He had a clipboard and rubber overshoes which sagged back with weight that bent his knees and pulled his shoulders back to balance his gut. In fevered preparation for his visit, I had scraped tomato-encrusted spinach off the maple hardwood that spans our main floor. In a different time and place, the maple hosted basketball games at the local junior high before a teacher had laid it over her slivered, gaping dining room fir. The shattered gym floor lines had been a kaleidoscope of green, blue, and red, which she sanded then applied a stain the colour of apple juice.

Two decades after that teacher's first gleeful steps over her smooth hardwood, Mat and I crossed it eagerly looking everywhere but down. The maple has since hosted baby showers and birthdays, wrestling matches and tag. It has loudly groaned while supporting dozens of friends for parties that occasionally end with me singing badly to the music of a jazz player on piano, a violinist on guitar, and a man hammering drums.

In spots, its boards are worn and exposed and these soft hollows hold memories of sounds: the bounce of my labour dance, the reverberating stomp of a child refusing to go to bed, the hollow echo of a child's head in a wrestling match gone wrong. I scrubbed what I could from the floor for this stranger on whom the next ten years of my life rested.

"How much do you want to rent this place for?" he asked and I told him the market rate.

The man from the bank drew the layout I love on grid paper. He didn't note the new south windows that filled the space with sunshine. It's a layout that provides views of my cedars, roses, and apples to the west and he didn't draw those either. He did, however, note the exterior's cracking, glass stucco, the rotting fascia, the screen door I have painted blue to eke out two more years of life. "You've got military shingles on that garage, eh?" He said while making marks on his paper. "Standing at attention, they are."

The man used my washroom then said, "You know you could help the slant in this floor?" He pointed under the dining table where milk regularly flowed towards the valley in the centre of our home. "You just need a telepost downstairs under the centre beam. Jack it up every three weeks or so and you'll level this floor out." I nodded and cursed his sense of balance that would soon fail him.

He headed up the stairs that even a hundred years ago couldn't have been up to code. Even in the absence of code, surely common sense would suggest that a foot-deep tread is a bad idea? Upstairs, he would have seen our half-storey's bedrooms and noted the laminate floors and absence of bedroom doors, which we had removed to save space. If he looked closely, he would have found the ancient gateways to rodent highways now deserted thanks to our cat.

I didn't see him fall, but I heard the crash of his tailbone on the slate landing. I heard the washboard sound of heavy cloth then a crack; the edge of my 100-year-old fir stair had caught his heel and its nose politely bowed in service. The man was embarrassed. He was also proud. Without thanks to my home's sacrifice, he said, "You really need some metal brackets or two by fours to secure the edges of these stairs."

I knew then that our house would fail market expectations. Two days later, he told the bank the house had very little value and the bank declined our request for a mortgage that perhaps may have crippled us, so I guess I should have been grateful our plans fell through. We had more money to buy a decent bottle of red wine sitting at the sun-washed dining table. Perhaps when the plum trees finally produce a heavy crop and the roses fully cover the pergola, we won't want to leave. Sure, we have more mornings to fight for the bathroom sink, to find privacy only in the basement, to put kids to bed like Jenga blocks. It can be done. For a century, it has been done and some days I wish the floors could tell me just how that family of eleven did it.

Of course, there was another option besides staying. We could have sold the house, but then we began to list what we would miss: my parents and our half dozen siblings are in walking distance, our neighbour Laura, the five playgrounds in a one-kilometre radius, the library, the Number 5 bus, our lilac, our quiet block, the Carrot, the buns at Popular Bakery that Madi can now be sent alone to buy, our apple tree. So we chose a third option: Mat and I moved downstairs. We left our scent and our bed, we left our pillows and side tables then parked ourselves in the basement on a terribly uncomfortable IKEA pull-out meant for (I now realize) one's most hated relatives. The three kids populated the bed we had abandoned sleeping horizontally and, for a month, we slept undisturbed except for the poor quality bed.

In time, we bought a bed, a mattress, and closet system. Our clothes moved downstairs and I managed to steal a pillow back from the kids so that when I lay back in the dark, quiet and cool of the basement, I fell asleep quickly and slept until morning without waking once.

The exterior of the house now has a fresh coat of yellow paint that holds up the crumbling stucco. It sports new windows and a stained-glass door that looks out on espaliered plums, wild roses and a garden that skirts the house in colour. Both toilets now flush anything we throw at them, which with Ali in the house can mean a box of OBS chased by a gallon of laundry detergent. Every other year, jumbles of electrical wire are replaced with slightly straighter new conduit. The garage has new shingles and since we kicked out the van (why should my automobile have shelter when my family needs more room?), it hosts Mat's music studio and our creative office from which I work standing at the thick pine window shelf. When I am typing there I see straight through the kitchen's patio door to the living room where regularly all three kids dance with varying degrees of nudity and really, they have plenty of room.

23

Canvassing 101

MADI CAME HOME PUMPED UP about a school project
sponsored by a bank that promised one lucky fourth grader an iPad. She
was determined to write an award-winning essay on the question: "How
can you make your community a better place to live?"

"I don't know what I'm going to say," she said with sudden self-
consciousness. Then she brightened, with an "I'll go ask the neighbours."

Lily and Alistair scrambled for coats and jackets as Madi collected a
pen and clipboard on which was a piece of eight by eleven white printer
paper. She had drawn a careful graph and on the left column she wrote,
"Address" and the second column she titled, "Notes." They worked their
way up the west side, then more cautiously up the east. They forbade me
from coming with them so I forbade them going into any fenced yards
to be mauled by dogs. Madi recorded their work and some were marked
"away" and others' answers were neatly added: "No dogs allowed in the
front yard" and "Watch out for each other's houses." I lurked around the
front of our house with my coffee and every time I came too close, Ali
acted tough, yelling in his toddler voice, "No Adults...NO ADULTS."

When they had knocked on every front door without a closed front
gate, they raced home, Madi's green knit sweater from Grandma dragging

on the ground behind her, collecting browning elm leaves. Inside she transferred the answers to a sheet in list form, and then set up my laptop. Working slowly, every couple of minutes she loudly announced her word count and my professional writer's heart swelled. As I folded laundry she read out her first draft:

HOW TO MAKE THE COMMUNITY A BETTER PLACE TO LIVE
By Madi Halton

I think there should be more senior homes, health care and dental around the community. I think every week a police should check on your street and keep you safe. Not only should cars drive slower around schools but on streets around any neighbourhoods. Lots of families can't afford homes so I think there should be bigger chances of owning (staying in) a home. There is a lot of littering in the communities and I think that should stop, and more garbage and recycling containers put up all around the areas. Cars might be having trouble to see in the dark so more light-posts should be put up in the communities, or even neighbourhoods. Lots of parks have sand and I think that is a little unsafe for small children because some like to eat sand and /or put it in their mouth. I also think kids should be involved with big or small events. There should be more family festivals and activities, because you can get to know your neighbour(s) better, and places on the block. A good neighbourhood is where your neighbours care for you by helping you with raking the leaves on your property and sometimes watches your house when you are gone. I also think kids should be allowed to vote! *We would help the environment, they would charge higher taxes for schools and make the Community a better place!!!*

I love this community and I want other people to like it too! As all communities, changes should be made in all sorts of ways. But I think everyone deserves to live somewhere, and I recommend my community. I recommend it because so many people around are very kind and respectful to me and my family.

When I asked her if I could print her essay in my book she said, "No."

"Please, I'll pay you," I said.

"How much?" She softened.

"One cent a word," I offered.

"No way, that's not enough," she said as she walked away.

"Ok, five cents a word, for 250 words, that's good money!" She was as good at math as she was at writing.

"Like fifteen dollars?" We shook on it and I can report that I paid good money to share with you the hopes of a little girl for her neighbourhood.

24

The Pendulum Swings

ON THE NORTHEAST EDGE of downtown Edmonton, the capital of Alberta and gateway to Canada's energy sector, Alberta Avenue has struggled since the car became King of Transport and the city expanded like its residents' waistlines: homeowners, money, and respect bloating out to the margins. This central community was old, cracked, and chipped. The suburbs were new, shiny, and smooth and so, as focus shifted elsewhere, what was already old decayed further.

As all fashions must come and go, the inner cores of cities across North America are becoming cool again thanks to cultural shifts that value shorter commutes, public transportation, and urban life. Improved downtown nightlife and lower housing prices in cities that are becoming, generally, unaffordable are major drivers drawing middle class folks back to older parts of the city, trading the occasional exchange with a drug addict for proximity to downtown.

Renewal in Alberta Avenue has been slow. Just walk along 118th Avenue and the ghosts of efforts past stand as a cautionary tale: two-dimensional metal sports figures act as colourful flags on the lamp standards, life-sized metal sculptures of volleyball players welcome walkers heading north on 93rd Street, and at the traffic circle on 101st Street, a metal baseball bat the height of my house stands surrounded by a circle of cement benches, all part of a failed exercise to brand Alberta Avenue with a sports theme.

When we first moved here, a quality-of-life report was released by the city of Edmonton and Alberta Avenue received a big fat zero, raising the ire of many of my neighbours. It affirmed everything everybody else in the city thought about the neighbourhood while it completely missed measuring many residents' actual lived experience found in any edition of the *Rat Creek Press*. Over the years the community newspaper has chronicled the issues, but perhaps more importantly the many active groups and programs that make life here great. Some, like the Sing, Sign, Laugh and Learn at Sprucewood Library have been going on for years. Others are newer, like the free Zumba sessions every Monday night in the community gardens behind the League. There are free group guitar lessons at Eastwood Community Hall, and the dog-walkers continue to walk together and are always open to new members. Plant exchanges, book clubs, parent meet-ups and seniors' teas. Plays and concerts, drive-in movies and Nordic poling, there is so much good.

While our neighbourhood had people willing to volunteer their time and skills, Alberta Avenue needed help to fund bigger projects to renew its tired infrastructure and fight some of the systemic policies and processes. Over the past decade Alberta Avenue has received millions of dollars from the city through the Alberta Avenue Initiative to upgrade 118th Avenue with new pavement, wide sidewalks, benches, and business facelifts. Through the process, residents were consulted on new zoning that would allow more density and, ideally, affordable housing that would replace some of the multiple-suite, unsafe rooming houses along the bus routes. The newest revitalization also funded a staff person who coordinated resident committees that discussed solutions to critical problems and distributed grant funds to help creative solutions happen. Like the ill-named group called CRUD (Community Response to Urban Disorder) that organized a weekly dog-walking club and started a monthly dinner club where neighbours visited local restaurants. The local non-profit Arts on the Ave started Kaleido, and then opened the Carrot Community Arts Coffeehouse where in the early days, Mat, my sister-in-law and I would barista every Tuesday taking turns bouncing baby Madi and making lattes. And to support my many neighbours who can't afford to get their large couches and mattress items to the dump, which requires a truck and money, the annual Big Bin Clean-Up offered to remove large items for a low fee.

The Broken Windows theory of policing was frequently discussed in the initial Alberta Avenue Initiative meetings. The theory is built around the idea that people will respond in kind to their environment. If a public space is beautiful, people will treat it with respect. If litter is cleaned up, it will accumulate more slowly and conversely, if a window is broken, then other windows will be broken faster and becomes tantamount to a Welcome Home sign to squatters.

Funding was also available for creative art projects. Along one alley that had a significant number of police calls, the dumpsters were painted with eyes. Murals appeared, like the one of locally beloved gardening author Lois Hole carrying a basket of flowers into a wall of sun-lit blue. Art of this kind has been painted on buildings that once were canvasses for low-level gang tags.

The police created Neighbourhood Teams that coordinated local volunteers, alongside community police, social workers and crime data nerds. Mat was part of a group that taught at-risk kids how to repair bikes, which brought them in contact with mentors and members of the police. The "We believe in 118" campaign asked all the Avenue businesses to stop selling nunchucks and drug paraphernalia and in exchange our family and many neighbours rewarded them with our business. They launched ads on billboards along 118th Avenue, letters with script in massive font: "Dear 'john': We've let the police know, they have our back on this one."

Each campaign required gathering, community building, creative thinking. Each program required multiple levels of partners from neighbours to school staff to city workers which empowered many who felt there was nothing they could do.

But before we go too far down the road titled "Everybody Loves Revitalization!" I must clarify that not everyone does. Some of my neighbours argue that it's not us who have the problem, but that it's everyone else's *perception* that is the problem. To them, living in Alberta Avenue with its quirky family shops and hazy storefront windows is like Christmas dinner with one's slightly drunk, favourite uncle. He adds charm and honesty to the night where stilted conversation about pickles and stuffing would have been. His vulnerability sometimes makes you love him more.

For other neighbours—some who have lived here many years—they are tired of the bullshit. Of the weird hours at the shops, of the mattresses with bloated bed bugs in the alley, of their neighbours who can't seem to get their shit together to mow their damn front lawn. For them, Christmas dinner is over and they are reliant on their now-truly-drunk-and-dozing uncle to drive them to church at midnight. For my part, I like the uncle. I can acknowledge that he needs some treatment, but the role he plays at the table (when and if he's not hurting someone) is important. In this neighbourhood there aren't only divergent views about the problem, but also about the "treatment"—if any—that Alberta Avenue needs now.

While change is slow, it's happening despite the debate. Since we moved to the neighbourhood fourteen years ago, the main street of 118th Avenue has been freshly paved and in some parts the cement has been dyed and scored to look like red brick. Many businesses have taken advantage of matching grants for facelifts, like the belly dance studio that beautifully tiled its entire front entrance. There are fewer prostitutes, though this could have more to do with easy tricks through the Internet, and more young families partially driven by the fact that one can buy a house here for less than anywhere else in the city. Public art, new restaurants, and popular festivals have brought life to some parts—though not all—of the street that were gaunt and hollow-eyed due to absentee landlords.

Many of the shops that are opening cater to the growing African community in the city. Every day of the week women in colourful dress do business at Mama Afro's Beauty Salon while their men saunter in and out of shops like the Bullie Barber/Driving School. At the Kasoa Tropical Food Market, palm oil and cassava can be bought inexpensively, and at Koultures fufu is served most nights of the week.

Sometimes I try to make friends with the shopkeepers in the myriad of small halal shops. As I bought falafel in a box one afternoon, I asked the owner if he lived around here. He laughed, "Oh no! We live up in Castledowns. Oh no." In fact, he wanted to emphasize the point so badly that he waved his arms frantically in front of himself as though I had offered him a joint as a cop passed. "We don't live near here," he repeated.

As with most change comes social tension. I was walking one morning with the girls to the playground and on the lamppost, just above the button for the walk signal, was a sign. Its Sharpie font shouted at me: GENTRIFICATION IS THE NEW COLONIALISM. Bolded and high-lighted, the sign's message captured my central fear about the change occurring here, of which I am a contributing part: if not thoughtfully done, we risk an over-reaching; that in aiming for safer back alleys, clean parks, and vibrant streets, our neighbourhood will become so desirable that its current culture and personality will disappear.

At its worst, gentrification and its corresponding lack of affordability is about displacement of the immigrant, the disabled, the low-income senior, the working class, the non-profit worker, the single-parent families. Bill would have to move; George who is blind and works at the Carrot would have to move; Siena would never have been able to afford her place if she was starting out again in Canada; my sister-in-law would still be renting; my cousin's community house wouldn't have started here; roughly ninety percent of the students in Madi's school wouldn't be there.

In the worst-case scenario, my family becomes a threat. By fixing up our home and our yard, by our activism, we run the risk of increasing property values on our street, which could lead to major affordability issues in the decades to come. It's an irony and a responsibility that every caring newcomer to a community should hold with consciousness and care.

At the end of the day, however neighbourhoods are very much like the humans that inhabit them, boasting life cycles with life stages: each claiming a certain beauty that ought to be respected. Each stage has its unique diseases too: chicken pox in childhood, H P V in early adulthood, tendonitis in one's thirties, gout in one's fifties, arthritis, then dementia. So too does each stage have its unique antidotes and interventions.

While some will define Alberta Avenue's life stage only by its disease, my family has seen its life. I have learned that despite appearances, shiny and new has its disadvantages while chipped and cracked has its beauties; all communities, old and new, have to work to be vital. We ignore this lesson at our cities' peril.

Epilogue

FOR ALL THE PEOPLE in my neighbourhood that this book
has introduced, I am keenly aware of those who are not represented
on these pages. The newcomer story is a complex and varied one and
while the Italians and then the Portuguese represented earlier waves,
Ethiopians, Somalis and Ghanaians now begin their lives and businesses
here. I didn't introduce you to the challenging small p-politics of running
a Farmers' Market or the campaign to demolish Cromdale Hotel.

When I look back at all that Mat and I wanted to achieve moving in
to this neighbourhood, we got a whole lot more and a little bit less than
we hoped. We wanted neighbours who could teach us. We wanted to
respond to the needs in our city in a more community-oriented way. How
we expected this to play out was unclear, but there was a sense that we
would bump into people on the street, chat, and suddenly find ourselves
sharing our food potluck-style with kids and dogs cheerily decorating the
perimeters of these dreams.

In reality, while we meet many people in the park, in line at the
Shoppers Drug Mart, at the entrance of the school, when it comes to
bringing people who check different boxes than me on the census home,
it's a whole lot more difficult. Outside of the growing and diverse group

of friends my children have, Mat and I continue to share life with a very small circle of people who are a lot like us. That's not to say that living in a diverse community hasn't changed us. It has, but it's a lot more about my perception changing than my close-knit circles of support rapidly diversifying.

The lifecycle of Alberta Avenue will continue to bring change and, if Mat gets his new electrical panel someday, we may or may not continue to be part of it. However, as long as I bike along these shaded streets, ride the Number 5 bus sitting next to Betty from next door, buy bread from Popular Bakery and eat flautas at El Rancho, I will be thankful for a neighbourhood that has taught me that shitty really is how you see it.

Acknowledgements

THIS BOOK WOULD BE A SLIM ONE indeed without those individuals who shared their stories with me. Abundant thanks to each of you named in the pages of this work for making this neighbourhood such a wonderful place to live and learn.

Thank you to all of the readers who contributed to the cuts and edits that made these stories so much better: Terri Wilson (my mom who read almost every iteration!), Kerrie Miller, Natasha Nunn, Trisha Estabrooks, Tina Faiz, Marilyn Hooper, Doug Wilson, Jeff and Ruth King, and my writing group pals: Danielle Metcalf-Chenail, Caitlin Crawshaw, Michael Lithgow, Erin McGregor.

I am a writer who needs a team because I like to brainstorm out loud about structure and also I don't care about grammar or spelling, so for all their work I thank my editors for their heavy lifting: Erinne Sevigny, Kimmy Beach and Maya Fowler-Sutherland.

Thank you to the team at the University of Alberta Press: Peter Midgley for taking a chance and reading the first version of the manuscript. And throughout the publishing process, thanks to the UAP team.

The financial support of the Edmonton Arts Council afforded me childcare and retreat space so these essays could be first drafted. The work the Council does in supporting Edmonton artists has directly and indirectly supported many who make Alberta Avenue their home. I am grateful.

Finally, I extend my great love to my family who continued to live with me despite that I was writing about their lives too. Mat, Madi, Lily, Alistair—thank you.

Sources

The obituary in "Unlikely Space Flight" is from a website called Your Life
Moments, accessed July 2, 2017, http://yourlifemoments.ca/sitepages/
obituary.asp?oid=542248.

The quote by Karlie85 in "Avoid this Place at Night" appeared online
in March 2014, yet the article has been removed since. Subsequent
editions of this book will include the authorial information should it
be found.

In "Rub and Tug in the City," the vignette in the final section previously
appeared in Halton, Carissa, "A Different Kind of Simikanis," in
Eighteen Bridges, Spring 2015, 22-44.

In "We Are All in This Together," Cheryl Whiskeyjack's vision of the
Kahkiyaw program was also published in the following essay: Halton,
Carissa, "Lost Fires Still Burn,' in *In This Together: Fifteen Stories of Truth
and Reconciliation*, ed. D. Metcalfe-Chenail (Victoria: Brindle and Glass,
2016), 159-70.

Other Titles from The University of Alberta Press

The rose that grew from concrete
Teaching and Learning with Disenfranchised Youth
DIANE WISHART
Qualitative research with interviews of at-risk inner-city students reveal the humanity behind the statistics.

Edmonton In Our Own Words
LINDA GOYETTE &
CAROLINA JAKEWAY ROEMMICH
Citizens with diverse viewpoints describe important events in Edmonton's development through written records and spoken stories.

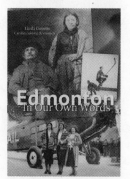

Street Sex Work and Canadian Cities
Resisting a Dangerous Order
SHAWNA FERRIS
De-stigmatization of sex work encourages efforts toward legal changes to create safe communities for all.

More information at www.uap.ualberta.ca

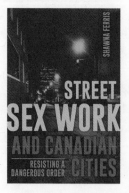